Why My Brain Hates Me?

Retrain The Brain
Get Rid Of Racing Thoughts
Have Your Brain Work For You

Harrison S. Mungal, Ph.D, Psy.D

Why My Brain Hates Me?

Copyright © 2024 Harrison S. Mungal

All rights reserved. Neither this publication nor any part of this publication may be reproduced or transmitted in any form or by any means, electronic or mechanical, including photocopying, recording or any information storage and retrieval system, without permission in writing from the author.

Contact author via email: info@harrisonmungal.com
info@agetoage.ca
www.agetoage.ca
www.harrisonmungal.com
www.harrisonmungalbooks.com
Facebook: Harrison Mungal
Twitter: AgeToAgeInc1
LinkedIn: Harrison Mungal, Ph.D., PsyD
YouTube: Harrison Mungal
Phone: 905-533-1334

ABOUT *the* AUTHOR

With an extensive background in clinical psychology, Harrison is deeply committed to enhancing the lives of those he counsels. His academic credentials are impressive, boasting dual doctoral degrees in Clinical Psychology and Philosophy in Social Work and two master's degrees in Social Work and Counselling. He also holds a Bachelor's degree in Theology. His areas of expertise encompass mental health, addiction, marital and relationship, family dynamics, and parenting issues.

Recognized as a leading authority in cognitive therapy, Harrison is a sought-after presenter at workshops. His multifaceted role allows him to assist individuals, couples, families, and corporations. Harrison, a global public speaker, has addressed audiences in over 42 countries at various conferences, seminars, and public events. His reach extends to radio and television appearances and he has authored over 30 books. He is widely respected for his profound insights, as well as his engaging sense of humour and enthusiasm for subjects like mental health, addictions, relationships, and parenting.

Harrison's approach to his work is both inventive and grounded in scientific principles. This unique methodology has earned him a sterling reputation, along with multiple awards and accolades from an array of institutions, including law enforcement agencies, municipal governments, community leaders, and corporate executives. He offers training and consultations to a diverse range of community partners, including medical professionals, social workers, first responders, law enforcement officials, and senior management teams.

An active participant in cognitive research, Harrison has led several groundbreaking studies aimed at aiding people with mental health issues like addiction, psychosis, anxiety, and depression. Among these studies are explorations into music therapy for schizophrenia, vaccination protocols for young children, and the role of substance abuse in the food service industry. His work on Thought Developmental Practice (TDP) has been particularly notable for providing alternative treatments for conditions like substance abuse, anxiety, PTSD, and depression.

With over two decades of professional experience, Harrison has worked with a broad and diverse range of populations. His experience encompasses 17 years in the mental health and psychiatry fields and more than a decade as a practicing clinical psychotherapist. He has provided services to a myriad of communities, including those affected by Acquired Brain Injuries, refugees, victims of warfare, and individuals in crisis across various settings, which include collaborations with police forces, hospitals, community agencies, and inpatient mental health facilities.

In terms of therapeutic approaches, Harrison is well-versed in a wide array of evidence-based treatments. These include, but are not limited to, Cognitive Behavioral Therapy (CBT), Cognitive Processing Therapy (CPT), Dialectical Behavioral Therapy (DBT), and Acceptance and Commitment Therapy (ACT). He is also skilled in Interpersonal Therapy (IPT), Motivational Interviewing Techniques, Grounding Techniques, and various other specialized forms of treatment, such as Humanistic Experiential Therapy and Psychodynamic Therapy.

Author: Harrison S. Mungal.

TABLE Of CONTENT

ABOUT THE AUTHOR 3

INTRODUCTION 7

THE POWERHOUSE CALLED THE BRAIN 9

THE BRAIN'S EMOTIONAL PROCESSING UNIT 17

THOUGHT, FEELING, CONTROL AND LEARNING 25

THE INNER BATTLEFIELD 55

SELF-CONCEPT 65

NEGATIVE THOUGHTS 71

REGRETS, FLAWS, AND WEAKNESSES 77

ANGER, FRUSTRATION, AND TEMPER 93

ANXIETY AND STRESS 99

UNHEALTHY DESIRES, ADDICTIONS, AND CRAVINGS 115

CONCLUSION 129

INTRODUCTION

"Why My Brain Hates Me?" is a book that will navigate you to the complex maze of neural processes, emotional intricacies, and cognitive challenges that we all face. This book aims to empower you with the knowledge and tools to take charge of your mental well-being. By exploring the mechanics of the brain, the origins of emotions, and the intricacies of self-control, among other topics, you'll understand not just what makes you tick but how you can tick better.

The brain is an extraordinary organ that serves as the command center for our thoughts, emotions, and actions. Yet, most of us go through life with only a vague understanding of how it operates, particularly in areas that affect our emotional well-being. By learning the science behind phenomena like negative thought patterns, emotional highs and lows, and psychological triggers, we can arm ourselves with the tools to make informed choices that enhance our mental health and overall quality of life.

Get ready for an engaging exploration that will take you through the building blocks of neural power, the complexities of emotional regulation, and the mechanics of thought formation. You'll also delve into often-overlooked topics like the mental battles that disrupt our peace of mind, the origins and impacts of self-perception, and strategies for managing mental health red flags. Along the way, you'll discover actionable insights and evidence-based practices that can transform your relationship with your brain.

While this book is grounded in scientific research and evidence-based practices, it is designed to be accessible. The intent is to provide a resource that balances factual rigour with readability, making the complex subject matter approachable. The topics are organized to create a seamless narrative flow, helping you connect the dots between what may initially seem like disparate elements of brain function and psychology.

As you progress through the chapters, you'll find a mix of scientific explanations, real-world anecdotes, and practical tips aimed at improving your understanding of why your brain behaves the way it does—and how you can make it work better for you. By the end, the goal is for you to have not only a deeper understanding of your brain but also a toolkit for enhancing your mental and emotional well-being.

So, let's begin this fascinating exploration into the realms of the human mind. There's much to uncover, and the key to a better understanding yourself and your potential for personal growth lies in the pages ahead.

THE POWERHOUSE *Called* the **BRAIN**

The brain is often likened to a supercomputer, but in reality, it's much more than that. Unlike any machine invented by humans, the brain has the ability to learn, adapt, and evolve. At the core of this incredible power are two key components: its functional anatomy and the neurotransmitters that serve as the brain's chemical messengers. Understanding these building blocks can help us better grasp the impact of our thoughts on our lives, both positive and negative, and understand "Why My Brain Hates Me."

When we talk about the brain's functional anatomy, we're essentially referring to how different parts of the brain are responsible for different aspects of who we are and how we function. These regions don't operate in isolation; instead, they communicate and collaborate in intricate ways that scientists are still working to fully understand. Below, we'll delve deeper into some key areas that have a significant impact on your emotions, thoughts, and overall mental well-being.

The prefrontal cortex, situated at the front of your brain, serves as your cognitive control center. It's responsible for what psychologists refer to as "executive functions," which include decision-making, problem-solving, and regulating emotional responses. When you're weighing the pros and cons of a difficult decision or trying to keep your emotions in check during a heated discussion, it's your prefrontal cortex that's hard at work. This region helps you act in accordance with long-term goals rather than succumbing to impulsive desires or emotional whims.

If the prefrontal cortex is the executive director, the amygdala is the emotional core of your brain. Located deep within the temporal lobes, this small, almond-shaped cluster of nuclei is crucial for emotional processing. Your amygdala triggers the sudden flush of love when you see a family member or the spike of fear when you hear an unexpected noise in the night. Its interplay with other brain regions, particularly the prefrontal cortex, helps you evaluate whether that unexpected noise is something dangerous that requires immediate action or just a harmless sound that can be ignored.

Nestled within the medial temporal lobe, the hippocampus plays a critical role in the formation of new memories and is also associated with learning and emotions. Think of it as your brain's filing system. Every piece of information you need to remember—academic, practical, or emotional—is processed here. A well-functioning hippocampus enables you to recall past experiences, both good and bad, and use them to navigate present challenges.

Though primarily associated with motor control, the cerebellum also contributes to cognitive functions such as attention and language and regulates fear and pleasure responses. Located just above the brainstem and beneath the cerebral hemispheres, it's involved in coordinating voluntary movements like posture, balance, and speech, ensuring that your body moves harmoniously and efficiently.

Situated deep within the cerebral hemispheres, the basal ganglia work with other brain regions to control complex actions and high-order thinking. They are crucial for habit formation, reward processing, and decision-making. Whenever you automatically reach for your toothbrush in the morning or feel a sense of satisfaction after completing a challenging task, it's the basal ganglia at play.

In short, the brain's functional anatomy is a marvel of biological engineering, and understanding how its various parts contribute to your thoughts, emotions, and actions offers a foundational basis for mental mastery. This knowledge equips you with the tools to better interpret why you feel the way you do, why you make confident choices, and how you can optimize these processes for a more fulfilling life.

If you've ever wondered why a piece of chocolate can lift your spirits or why a good workout makes you feel euphoric, you have neurotransmitters to thank. These remarkable chemicals are the silent puppet masters of your brain, pulling the strings that dictate your mood, thoughts, and even your behaviour. But what exactly are neurotransmitters, and how do they wield tremendous power over our mental state?

Neurotransmitters are essentially the language of your brain. They're the chemicals that neurons, or brain cells, use to communicate with each other. Think of them as the postal service of your nervous system: they deliver messages from one neuron to another, dictating everything from whether you feel elated, sad, energized, or relaxed. These messages can either excite or inhibit actions from taking place, allowing for complex responses to various situations.

Among the many neurotransmitters, a few stand out for their significant impact on mood and thought. Let's consider three of the most influential ones.

Dubbed the 'feel-good' neurotransmitter, dopamine is crucial for sensations of pleasure and satisfaction. It's released during enjoyable activities like eating, socializing, and accomplishing tasks. It's also intricately tied to motivation; lower levels of dopamine can make even simple tasks feel laborious.

Serotonin is a jack of all trades. It regulates mood and is vital for sleep, appetite, and even digestion. Imbalanced levels are often linked with mood disorders. For instance, a deficiency in serotonin is commonly associated with feelings of depression.

Norepinephrine acts like the alarm bell of your brain. It plays a pivotal role in your body's stress response, preparing you to face challenging situations. While essential for survival, chronic high levels can result in anxiety and stress disorders.

Maintaining the right balance of these neurotransmitters is akin to fine-tuning an intricate machine. Too much or too little of any one chemical can throw off your entire system. For example, excessive dopamine release is observed in certain forms of psychosis, while deficient levels are linked with conditions like Parkinson's disease. Similarly, an overflow of norepinephrine can lead to stress and anxiety, while insufficient amounts may result in lethargy and low energy.

Our lifestyle choices—what we eat, how much we exercise, and even how well we sleep—can influence neurotransmitter activity. A diet rich in fruits, vegetables, and lean protein can provide the precursors needed for neurotransmitter synthesis. Physical activity, on the other hand, boosts the release of endorphins, often called natural mood lifters, and can also regulate levels of stress-related neurotransmitters. Even the quality of our sleep has a say in this biochemical equation, with poor sleep linked to imbalances in serotonin and dopamine.

Understanding neurotransmitters enables us to grasp why we react the way we do in different situations and why certain imbalances can lead to specific mood disorders. This knowledge provides us with the power to make informed decisions that can positively affect our mental well-being. Whether choosing a nutrient-rich meal, engaging in regular physical activity, or prioritizing good sleep, small lifestyle changes can make a big difference in achieving a balanced neurotransmitter profile, setting the stage for better emotional and mental health.

Now that we've touched on the brain's functional anatomy and neurotransmitters let's explore their relevance to our everyday lives. One area where their impact is most felt is in the realm of positive and negative thinking. Your thoughts have the power to influence neurotransmitter activity, which in turn affects your mood, your actions, and even your physical well-being.

When we dwell on negative thought patterns, the impact on our mental, emotional, and even physical well-being can be more profound than we might initially realize. The cascade of biochemical reactions set off by negative thinking doesn't just alter your mood in the short term; it can also have long-lasting implications that extend far beyond a bad day or a momentary lapse in emotional well-being.

From a neurological standpoint, constantly engaging in negative thoughts can strengthen specific neural pathways in the brain, almost like a river carving out a canyon over time. Neuroscientists often summarize this phenomenon with the phrase "neurons that fire together, wire together." Essentially, the more you entertain negative thoughts, the more robust those neural pathways become, making it easier for your brain to access and perpetuate these thoughts in the future. This self-perpetuating cycle can make it increasingly challenging to break free from a negative mindset, leading to a sort of "cognitive rut."

On an emotional level, chronic negativity can lead to a reduced capacity for experiencing joy and happiness. It's as if your emotional spectrum becomes constricted, with feelings like hope, enthusiasm, and gratitude making fewer and fewer appearances in your daily life. Over time, this can manifest as chronic low mood or even contribute to clinical conditions like depression and anxiety disorders.

The effects of sustained negative thinking aren't limited to your mind; they also extend to your body. As mentioned earlier, negative thoughts often trigger the release of stress hormones like cortisol. While cortisol is useful in acute, short-term situations—like running away from a predator—in the long term, elevated levels can wreak havoc on your body. You might experience sleep disturbances, weight gain, high blood pressure, and a weakened immune system, making you more susceptible to illnesses.

The social ramifications are equally noteworthy. People are naturally drawn to positivity and can be repelled by consistent negativity. If you're always emanating negative energy, you may find your social circle shrinking or relationships suffering. Over time, this social isolation can exacerbate feelings of loneliness and sadness, creating a vicious cycle that further entrenches your negative thought patterns.

Finally, a negative mindset can act like blinders, limiting your view of the world and constricting your sense of what's possible. Opportunities for personal growth, career advancement, and meaningful relationships might go unnoticed or be dismissed outright as your brain becomes conditioned to expect failure or disappointment.

While the downsides of negative thinking can be severe and far-reaching, the benefits of positive thinking are equally potent and transformative. When you cultivate a habit of positive thinking, the ripple effects touch every facet of your life, from your neurological functioning to your emotional well-being, physical health, social interactions, and opportunities for growth.

Positive thoughts actively engage and reshape your brain's neural architecture. Just as negative thoughts strengthen specific pathways that lead to a vicious cycle of pessimism, positive thoughts do the opposite. They reinforce neural pathways associated with happiness, resilience, and well-being, making it easier for your brain to travel along these routes in the future. This phenomenon, often termed "neuroplasticity," allows your brain to adapt in a way that makes positive thinking more of a default setting than a conscious effort.

The emotional payoffs of a positive mindset are manifold. With increased levels of neurotransmitters like dopamine and serotonin, you're more likely to experience feelings of happiness, contentment, and relaxation. The world starts to appear less as a hostile or indifferent place and more as an environment filled with potential and promise. You'll find that joy and gratitude become more frequent visitors in your emotional repertoire, enriching your day-to-day experience of life.

A growing body of research backs the physiological benefits of positive thinking. Lower levels of stress hormones contribute to better sleep, a more robust immune system, and even improved cardiovascular health. Positivity not only enhances the quality of your life but can also extend its duration.

On a social level, positivity has a magnetic quality. People are naturally attracted to individuals who exude positive energy, creating a virtuous circle where your positive mindset draws others toward you, further enhancing your sense of well-being. Healthy relationships are foundational to emotional health, and a positive outlook can improve your interpersonal interactions, leading to stronger bonds and a more fulfilling social life.

A positive mindset doesn't just make life more enjoyable; it also broadens your perspective and enhances your problem-solving abilities. This expanded worldview enables you to identify opportunities you might have previously overlooked or discounted. Whether it's taking on new responsibilities at work, pursuing a long-held passion, or deepening personal relationships, a positive attitude can be the catalyst for meaningful change and growth in your life.

Cultivating positive thought patterns is more than just a feel-good philosophy; it's a strategic approach to improving multiple dimensions of your life. Through the subsequent chapters, we'll delve into actionable strategies rooted in scientific evidence and real-world applications aimed at helping you shift your mindset.

The goal is to arm you with the knowledge and tools needed to transition from understanding your brain's immense power to harnessing it for a life of greater fulfillment and well-being. As we'll see in the chapters ahead, understanding the powerhouse that is your brain is the first step in mastering it. And mastery, as you'll soon discover, is not just about control; it's about harmonizing with this incredible organ to live a more fulfilling life.

THE BRAIN'S *Emotional* PROCESSING UNIT

As we transition from understanding the brain's foundational role in shaping our thoughts to its complex responsibilities in emotional regulation, it's important to recognize the interwoven nature of these functions. This gives us a better understanding of "Why My Brain Hates Me." Just as your thoughts can significantly impact your mood and emotional well-being, so too can your emotional state influence your thought patterns and decision-making abilities. Indeed, emotions are not just by-products of our experiences but are integral forces that shape them. They act as both navigational tools and warning signals, guiding us through the complexities of social interactions, personal relationships, and even our inner dialogues.

In this chapter, we'll peel back the layers on one of the brain's most fascinating and, at times, perplexing domains—emotions. We'll start by defining emotions and then probe into their origins. We'll explore how our brains exert control over our emotional states, what happens when that control slips, and why gaining mastery over our emotional landscape

THE BRAIN'S EMOTIONAL PROCESSING UNIT

is not just a quest for happiness but a journey toward a more fulfilling life.

Emotions are more than just fleeting feelings or momentary moods; they are complex psychological states involving a symphony of physiological, cognitive, and behavioural components. While they may seem intangible or elusive, emotions are rooted in tangible processes within the brain. They act as a bridge between your internal world and the external environment, guiding your interactions, shaping your perceptions, and influencing your decision-making.

When discussing emotions, we often think of love, joy, anger, sadness, and fear. But in reality, our emotional landscape is far more intricate and nuanced. Each emotion you experience is like a unique colour, created by mixing different shades of physiological responses, cognitive assessments, and behavioural reactions. This intricate palette colours every aspect of your life, from your most mundane activities to your most significant life events.

Understanding the nature of emotions—the what, why, when, where and how—is the first step in mastering them. As we explore further, we'll delve into the origins of emotions, how the brain orchestrates them, and the implications of this complex interplay for your daily life and overall well-being.

The origins of our emotions are deeply rooted in both the biology of our brains and the experiences we go through, creating a fascinating interplay between nature and nurture. While it might be tempting to consider emotions as purely abstract or psychological constructs, they are, in fact, grounded in authentic and complex neurobiological processes.

Various regions of the brain contribute to the tapestry of our emotional experiences. One of the key players is the amygdala, often considered the brain's emotional command center. Located deep within the brain, this small, almond-shaped cluster of nuclei is instrumental in the initial recognition and processing of emotional stimuli. Then there's the prefrontal cortex, the brain's executive suite, which helps regulate these emotional responses, adding a layer of cognitive control.

But that's not all. The hippocampus, involved in memory formation, often ties emotions to specific memories, which can be triggered by certain stimuli. Additionally, other brain regions like the insular cortex and the ventromedial prefrontal cortex also participate in generating and modulating emotions, showing just how elaborate the neural underpinnings of our emotional experiences really are.

We can't discuss the origins of emotions without mentioning the crucial role of neurotransmitters and hormones. Chemical messengers like dopamine, serotonin, and norepinephrine act as the couriers that transmit signals between neurons, enabling the emotional responses generated in one part of the brain to be communicated and acted upon by others. These neurochemical processes set the stage for the emotional experiences we eventually perceive consciously.

While the machinery for emotional experience is built into our neural architecture, the specific triggers often come from our environment. Social interactions, sensory experiences, and even cultural norms can all act as catalysts for emotional responses. For instance, a kind word from a friend might trigger feelings of happiness and warmth, while a looming work deadline could instigate stress and anxiety.

Our thoughts and beliefs play a decisive role in shaping our emotional landscape. Your cognitive interpretations of events can amplify, diminish, or even completely alter the emotions you experience. For example, if you interpret a friend's lack of communication as a sign they don't care about you, feelings of sadness or rejection may ensue. On the other hand, if you interpret the same behaviour as them being busy or going through a tough time, your emotional response could be entirely different.

THE BRAIN'S EMOTIONAL PROCESSING UNIT

The origins of emotions are multifaceted and intricately woven into the fabric of both our biological makeup and our personal experiences. The complex interplay between brain regions, neurotransmitters, external triggers, and cognitive evaluations creates the rich, multifaceted emotional lives we all lead. As we move forward, we'll explore how this powerful system of emotional generation and regulation can be both a source of remarkable personal strength and, at times, a challenge to master.

When we ponder the question of control in the context of brain function and emotions, it's not so much a matter of the brain exerting a dictatorial influence over us but rather acting as a sophisticated guidance system. This system integrates sensory information, past experiences, and future goals to generate emotional states, which in turn influence our thoughts, actions, and interactions.

The brain employs a network of interconnected regions to manage the multifaceted aspects of your emotional life. For instance, the amygdala's rapid emotional assessments are tempered by the prefrontal cortex's more rational analysis, providing a balanced emotional response. The hippocampus adds context by linking the current experience with relevant memories. This integrated process enables your brain to produce nuanced emotional reactions that are aligned not just with immediate circumstances but also with your long-term well-being.

Emotions serve as internal signposts that guide our behaviour. Feelings like fear, although uncomfortable, serve an essential function by signalling potential danger and preparing your body for quick action. Similarly, feelings of happiness or contentment often indicate that you're engaged in activities aligned with your values or beneficial to your well-being, subtly encouraging you to seek similar experiences in the future.

Neurotransmitters are not just messengers; they are also regulators. By modulating the intensity and duration of signals between neurons, neurotransmitters like dopamine, serotonin, and norepinephrine can amplify or dampen emotional experiences. This biochemical layer of control can influence everything from your ability to focus on a task to your willingness to engage in social activities.

While emotions often arise in response to external events, we have the cognitive tools to moderate them. This is where higher-order brain functions come into play. By employing strategies like cognitive reframing, mindfulness, or even simple distraction, you can exert a level of control over your emotional states. Essentially, your brain offers you a toolkit for emotional self-regulation, provided you know how to use it.

Beyond influencing our emotional states, the brain also governs a host of autonomic functions like heart rate, breathing, and digestion through the autonomic nervous system. This level of control is usually subconscious but serves to maintain homeostasis and overall physiological well-being, which indirectly impacts our emotional state.

Understanding the mechanisms through which our brains exert control can empower us to collaborate more effectively with this masterful system. Rather than feeling like passive subjects of our brain's whims, we can become active participants in shaping our emotional lives.

Having explored the intricate mechanisms by which our brains generate and regulate emotions, it's time to turn our attention to a pressing question: How can mastering control over our negative emotions lead to self-improvement? The answer is as multifaceted as the emotional processes themselves, with implications for our psychological well-being, physical health, social relationships, and personal growth.

One of the most immediate benefits of learning to control negative emotions is increased psychological resilience. When you understand how to regulate emotions like fear, anger, or sadness effectively, you're better equipped to face life's challenges without being overwhelmed. This form of emotional agility allows you to encounter setbacks and

THE BRAIN'S EMOTIONAL PROCESSING UNIT

obstacles with a balanced perspective, reducing the likelihood of spiralling into anxiety or depression.

Negative emotions can cloud judgment, making it difficult to see situations clearly or make rational decisions. By learning to control these emotional states, you improve your decision-making abilities. Whether choosing to walk away from a heated argument or making a significant life change like a career move, effective emotional regulation provides the mental clarity needed to assess situations objectively and make informed choices.

Our emotions don't exist in a vacuum; they affect our interactions with everyone around us. Poor control over negative emotions can strain relationships, leading to conflicts, misunderstandings, and, over time, potential isolation. Learning to manage these emotions fosters healthier social interactions. You become more empathetic, less reactive, and more adept at conflict resolution—traits that improve personal and professional relationships.

As previously discussed, sustained negative emotions can trigger physiological responses, like the release of stress hormones, that are detrimental to physical health. Learning to control these emotional states can have tangible health benefits. Reduced stress levels correlate with a lower risk of chronic conditions such as hypertension, diabetes, and heart disease. Even your immune system stands to benefit, making you more resilient to infections and illnesses.

Mastering emotional control can serve as a catalyst for broader personal development. A stable emotional state creates a conducive environment for introspection, self-assessment, and the pursuit of personal goals. Whether it's acquiring a new skill, enhancing productivity, or nurturing creativity, emotional stability provides the foundation upon which these aspirations can be built.

Finally, it's worth noting that learning to control negative emotions often leads to an amplification of positive ones. As you become more adept at mitigating emotional lows, you'll find that your emotional highs—moments of joy, enthusiasm, and fulfillment—become all the more pronounced and enriching. In essence, you're not just eliminating the negative; you're making room for more of the positive.

To surmise, gaining control over negative emotions is not just about avoiding discomfort; it's about unlocking a more fulfilling, healthy, and balanced life. The ripple effects of this mastery touch every facet of your existence, from the quality of your thoughts to the richness of your relationships and the pursuit of your life's ambitions.

THE BRAIN'S EMOTIONAL PROCESSING UNIT

THOUGHT, FEELING, CONTROL and LEARNING

As we venture further into the labyrinthine intricacies of the brain, this chapter aims to broaden our perspective by focusing on the brain's profound impact on our thoughts, feelings, control, and the fundamental learning process. This helps us understand "Why My Brain Hates Me." Having examined how the brain controls and processes our emotional states, it's crucial to explore how this control extends to our cognitive and educational experiences.

This chapter will not only dissect the concept of control in these broader dimensions but also highlight the symbiotic relationship between thinking and feeling. Through this exploration, we will uncover strategies for optimizing our mental well-being and grasp the transformative power of lifelong control.

The brain is not just an emotional control center; it's also the ultimate conductor of our thoughts and the facilitator of our learning experiences. These four aspects—thought, feeling, control and learning—are deeply interconnected, each influencing and being influenced by the others in a dynamic interplay.

At the core of our thought processes are complex neural pathways that form networks responsible for everything from solving a math problem to pondering life's existential questions. Regions like the prefrontal cortex play a pivotal role in cognitive control, helping us focus our attention, make decisions, and solve problems. Meanwhile, other areas like the parietal lobe help us process spatial and mathematical information, further contributing to the realm of conscious thought.

As we've already explored, the brain has specialized regions like the amygdala that serve as hubs for emotional processing and regulation. These emotional centers are in constant communication with cognitive regions, resulting in an intricate two-way street. For example, an emotional state like anxiety can cloud rational thinking, while disciplined cognitive strategies can be employed to manage emotional turmoil.

Control is a multifaceted process that involves several regions of the brain. For instance, the hippocampus is crucial for memory formation, an essential aspect of learning. The basal ganglia and the cerebellum play roles in skill acquisition and the formation of habits. And let's not forget the neurotransmitters, like dopamine, which signal the pleasure and reward associated with acquiring new knowledge or mastering a new skill, thus encouraging further learning.

The crux of this interconnected web is that each component—thought, feeling, control and learning—influences the others. A positive emotional state can enhance cognitive function and make control more effective. Conversely, the act of controlling something new can induce positive emotional states, fostering a feedback loop that benefits both cognitive and emotional well-being.

In the realm of neuroscience and psychology, the term "control" extends beyond its everyday usage to encompass a nuanced array of cognitive and emotional regulatory processes. It's not merely about willpower or restraint but involves a sophisticated network of neural interactions that guide our thoughts, emotions, and actions. Understanding control in this context provides us with the lexicon to explore its role in shaping our mental well-being, relationships, and overall life experience.

In the context of brain function, control refers to the brain's capacity to manage, direct, and regulate cognitive and emotional processes. This governance is not authoritarian but more akin to a democratic system where various brain regions contribute to the decision-making process. For instance, while the amygdala might signal a threat, leading to fear or anxiety, the prefrontal cortex assesses this input. It can override or modulate the emotional response based on a broader evaluation of context, past experience, and future objectives. This dynamic interplay exemplifies the brain's inherent control mechanisms, which are designed to yield balanced, adaptive responses to a wide array of situations.

Diving deeper into the neural foundations of control, we find a remarkable orchestra of brain regions and neurotransmitters working in concert to enable self-control and cognitive regulation. This complex neural machinery allows us to navigate the daily challenges and opportunities, from managing emotional responses to making ethical decisions or solving intricate problems. Understanding this neural basis empowers us to appreciate the exquisite intricacy of control mechanisms and, more importantly, to harness them effectively.

Located at the front of the brain, the prefrontal cortex is often likened to an executive control center. Its dorsolateral region is particularly crucial for cognitive functions like working memory, planning, and abstract reasoning. Meanwhile, the ventromedial area is more involved in value-based decision-making and emotional regulation. The prefrontal cortex's unique architecture, rich in neurotransmitter receptors, enables it to modulate emotional responses generated by other brain regions like the amygdala, thus serving as a cornerstone of self-control.

Situated just behind the prefrontal cortex, the anterior cingulate cortex serves as an internal error detection system. It is especially active when you're faced with conflicting information or choices, helping you resolve conflicts and make decisions. The anterior cingulate cortex is also involved in recognizing social norms and ethical considerations, making it a key player in moral and social forms of self-control.

Though primarily known for its role in generating emotional responses, the amygdala also contributes to emotional self-control by providing the raw emotional data that the prefrontal cortex and anterior cingulate cortex evaluate. It's the initial spark that can ignite an emotional fire, but it's also subject to the regulatory influences of these other regions, which can quell or fan the flames as needed.

The role of neurotransmitters in self-control and cognitive regulation is pivotal. Serotonin is often implicated in mood and impulse control, affecting how we respond to emotional triggers. Dopamine governs the brain's reward system, influencing our ability to delay gratification in pursuit of long-term goals. Noradrenaline, another key neurotransmitter, plays a role in alertness and the ability to focus, directly impacting cognitive control.

One of the most empowering aspects of the neural basis of control is its plasticity—the ability to adapt and change. The neural pathways associated with self-control can be strengthened through targeted mental exercises, mindfulness practices, or even pharmacological interventions. This adaptability offers a beacon of hope for those seeking to improve their self-control and cognitive regulation, demonstrating that lasting change is attainable with consistent effort and effective strategies.

Understanding the neural basis of self-control and cognitive regulation provides a window into one of the human brain's most complex and awe-inspiring faculties. As we proceed, we'll look at the dual aspects of control—its benefits and potential drawbacks—to better equip ourselves with the knowledge and tools to navigate the labyrinth of our cognitive and emotional lives.

The notion of control, especially within the context of brain function, is neither entirely positive nor wholly negative. It's a tool—a remarkably powerful one—that can be wielded to varying degrees of effectiveness depending on the situation, one's understanding of it, and the strategies employed. To fully grasp the concept of control, it's vital to appreciate its dual aspects, examining both its empowering benefits and its potential limitations or drawbacks.

Control, in its essence, is a double-edged sword. While its benefits in enhancing cognitive function, emotional well-being, and life outcomes are considerable, the potential drawbacks caution us against an unexamined or excessive application of control. As we continue to navigate through the intricate landscape of brain function, thought, and emotion, a nuanced understanding of control's dual aspects equips us with the wisdom to use this powerful tool judiciously.

While the concept of control within the brain's functioning has its complexities and potential drawbacks, it's crucial to delve into its empowering benefits in depth. These benefits are manifold, extending across cognitive, emotional, and social domains and even impacting our physical well-being. Understanding these advantages provides not just a theoretical appreciation of control but also offers actionable insights that can significantly improve various facets of our lives.

One of the most immediate cognitive benefits of control is the enhancement of attention and focus. By effectively regulating distracting thoughts and external stimuli, the brain's control mechanisms allow us to engage deeply with academic, professional, or creative tasks. This focused attention is crucial for success in a world filled with distractions.

Control mechanisms also extend to decision-making and problem-solving processes. With adequate control, the brain can better weigh options, evaluate risks, and foresee consequences, leading to decisions that are not only rational but also aligned with long-term objectives.

Control plays a pivotal role in emotional regulation, allowing us to effectively manage emotional highs and lows. Control mechanisms provide the levers for this vital emotional tuning, whether it's dampening the intensity of negative emotions like anger or anxiety or enhancing positive feelings like joy or satisfaction.

Over time, effective emotional regulation contributes to overall mental health. By managing emotional extremes and reducing the frequency of negative emotional states, control serves as a protective factor against mental health issues such as anxiety disorders, depression, and even some personality disorders.

Control mechanisms contribute significantly to emotional intelligence, which encompasses the ability to recognize, understand, and manage both one's emotions and the emotions of others. This form of intelligence is invaluable in building and maintaining relationships, both personal and professional.

Effective control extends to conflict resolution skills. By regulating emotional responses during heated situations, individuals can approach conflicts with a level head, allowing for constructive dialogue and mutual problem-solving rather than escalating tensions.

Control is a cornerstone of self-discipline, essential for the achievement of long-term goals. Whether adhering to a fitness regimen, pursuing higher education, or climbing the professional ladder, control mechanisms enable us to delay immediate gratification in favour of future rewards.

Control also contributes to resilience and adaptability, two key attributes in personal development. Effective control helps us bounce back from setbacks and adapt to new situations, furthering both our personal and professional growth.

Control mechanisms also extend to stress management, regulating the body's release of stress hormones like cortisol and adrenaline. Effective stress management has a direct positive impact on physical health, reducing risks of chronic conditions such as hypertension and heart disease.

Effective control also influences lifestyle choices, such as diet and exercise, contributing to long-term health and even potentially extending lifespan. Individuals can significantly impact their physical well-being by regulating impulses and making thoughtful choices.

While the advantages of control in cognitive and emotional regulation are well-documented and widely appreciated, it's crucial also to scrutinize the potential pitfalls. Control is not an unequivocal good; when misapplied or taken to an extreme, it can lead to a host of challenges that range from psychological distress to interpersonal difficulties and even physical health issues. Let's delve deeper into these less-discussed, darker facets of control to acquire a more balanced perspective.

One of the most insidious drawbacks of excessive control is emotional suppression. While it might seem advantageous to keep emotions like anger, sadness, or fear in check, consistently bottling up these feelings can lead to longer-term psychological issues, including increased stress and susceptibility to mental health conditions like anxiety and depression.

The pressure of maintaining an emotional facade can also lead to 'leakage' where suppressed emotions manifest in unintended ways, such as irritability or passive-aggressive behaviour.

When control translates into an inflexible mental approach, the result is cognitive rigidity. This narrow mindset can limit creativity, reduce problem-solving capabilities, and stifle innovation. In a rapidly evolving world that often requires adaptive thinking, cognitive rigidity is a significant handicap. It can affect not just professional success but also personal growth, preventing you from broadening your horizons or embracing new experiences.

Over-control can seep into social interactions, making them appear calculated or inauthentic. This impacts not just how you're perceived by others but also the quality of your relationships.

When interactions are governed by excessive control, they lack spontaneity and emotional depth, reducing the potential for genuine connection. This can lead to a cycle of social dissatisfaction, where relationships feel unfulfilling, reinforcing the perceived need for even more control.

Control often involves evaluating multiple options and making the best possible decision. However, an excessive focus on control can lead to a state of 'analysis paralysis,' where the fear of making the wrong choice hampers decision-making. This can be debilitating in scenarios that require prompt action and can generate significant stress, ultimately eroding self-confidence and decision-making abilities.

Maintaining high levels of control demands cognitive effort, which can lead to mental fatigue or 'ego depletion.' This drained state can reduce self-control in other areas, creating a counterproductive cycle. Moreover, the chronic stress associated with excessive control can manifest physically, elevating risks for conditions like hypertension, digestive issues, and weakened immune function.

Lastly, over-control can impede the learning process. A need to maintain control can make individuals less open to feedback and less willing to take the risks often necessary for learning and growth. This hampers adaptability, a quality increasingly crucial in both personal and professional spheres.

Understanding the potential drawbacks of control offers a more comprehensive view of this complex cognitive faculty. The objective isn't to diminish the value of control but to use this understanding as a catalyst for a more balanced, measured approach. It calls for a form of metacognition, where we think about how we think and control how we control, optimizing this powerful tool for our benefit while sidestepping its potential pitfalls.

Armed with a nuanced understanding of control's dual aspects—its remarkable benefits and its potential pitfalls—we can now turn our focus toward optimization. How can we modulate the level of control we exert over our thoughts and feelings for the best possible outcomes? The answer lies in a strategic approach that employs various cognitive techniques and practices designed to bring balance and adaptability to our emotional regulation and thought processes.

One of the most effective techniques for optimizing control is mindfulness, which involves cultivating awareness of the present moment without judgment. This practice helps us become aware of our thoughts and emotions as they arise, allowing for a more nuanced form of control that neither suppresses nor indulges them.

Another invaluable tool for balanced control is cognitive reframing, a technique that involves altering how we interpret events or emotions. Instead of viewing a situation as threatening, for example, we can reframe it as a challenge or an opportunity for growth, thus changing our emotional response and the level of control needed.

Behavioural activation is a strategy that involves identifying actions that induce positive emotional states and deliberately incorporating them into our routine. By doing so, we exert a form of proactive control over our emotional well-being rather than merely reacting to emotional states as they arise.

The simple act of labelling our emotions can significantly impact our ability to control them. By naming what we feel, we engage the prefrontal cortex and lessen the activation of the amygdala, allowing for a more measured emotional response.

A more advanced form of emotional labelling, emotional granularity, involves identifying emotions with a high degree of specificity. Instead of merely feeling "bad," one might recognize feelings of "disappointment," "resignation," or "melancholy." This nuanced understanding aids in applying the appropriate level of emotional control.

When faced with intense emotions, taking a brief pause before reacting can be remarkably effective. This technique creates a temporal distance between the emotional trigger and your response, allowing the brain's control mechanisms to intervene more effectively.

While much of control focuses on managing negative emotions, we can also exert control to amplify positive experiences. The act of savouring involves deliberately focusing on the positive aspects of an experience to enhance our emotional response, contributing to overall well-being.

By adopting these strategies and techniques, we can modulate the control we exert over our thoughts and feelings, achieving a balanced state that maximizes our cognitive potential and emotional well-being. It's about fine-tuning the dials, not flipping the switches—about mastering the art of control in a way that enriches, rather than constricts, our lives. This tailored approach allows us to navigate the complexities of human emotion and thought with agility, wisdom, and, most importantly, a sense of empowered control.

As we dive further into the mechanics of control, particularly in the realm of emotional regulation, it becomes imperative to clarify some often used but rarely differentiated terms: feelings and emotions. While these terms are frequently used interchangeably, understanding their distinctions can significantly enhance our control strategies.

Feelings are best understood as the conscious experiences that emanate from emotional states. They are the moment-to-moment manifestations of emotions that we can identify and articulate. For example, you might feel angry during an argument or elated after receiving good news. Feelings are highly situational, influenced by specific events, and tend to be short-lived, dissipating once the triggering situation is resolved or changes.

Feelings become apparent to us when we become consciously aware of them, often aided by the act of labelling, as discussed in the previous section. This awareness and articulation serve as a form of control, allowing us to manage the feeling effectively by either prolonging it, as in the case of happiness or contentment or mitigating it, as may be needed for feelings like anger or anxiety.

On the other hand, emotions are more complex, often enduring psychological states that arise from various factors, including our thoughts, physiological responses, and even long-standing beliefs or attitudes. Unlike feelings, emotions don't always manifest in ways we can easily identify or articulate. For example, a general sense of unease or irritability may actually be manifestations of a more complex emotion like stress or discontentment.

Emotions involve more extensive neural networks and cognitive processes compared to feelings. While feelings are typically processed in regions like the prefrontal cortex (where conscious awareness occurs) and the amygdala (which triggers immediate emotional responses), emotions engage a broader array of brain regions and neurotransmitter systems. They often involve intricate cognitive evaluations, memories, and moral or ethical considerations.

It's important to note that feelings and emotions are not mutually exclusive but parts of a continuum. Feelings can give rise to more complex emotions, and emotions can manifest as various feelings over time. Understanding this interplay can offer a more nuanced approach to emotional control. For instance, recognizing that a feeling of sadness is part of a broader emotional state of melancholy may lead to different coping strategies than treating it as an isolated, momentary experience.

THOUGHT, FEELING, CONTROL AND LEARNING

Distinguishing between feelings and emotions provides us with a more refined toolkit for emotional regulation and control. By understanding feelings as the situational, moment-to-moment experiences that they are and recognizing emotions as the complex, multi-faceted states that can endure and evolve, we gain the ability to navigate our emotional landscape with greater sophistication and efficacy. This nuanced understanding enriches our overall strategy for modulating control, allowing us to meet each emotional experience—be it a fleeting feeling or a pervasive emotion—with the most effective and adaptive response.

As we grapple with the intricacies of emotional control, it becomes increasingly vital to develop effective strategies for managing negative feelings. While our prior discussions have laid the groundwork for understanding control, feelings, and emotions, we now turn our focus to actionable techniques tailored to regulate negative feelings both in the immediate context and over the long term.

The 5-4-3-2-1 Grounding Technique, a simple yet powerful method, involves identifying five things you can see, four things you can touch, three things you can hear, two things you can smell, and one thing you can taste. This sensory grounding can quickly divert attention from negative feelings, providing immediate emotional relief.

Box Breathing also known as square breathing, this technique involves inhaling deeply for a count of four, holding the breath for another four counts, exhaling for four counts, and then holding the breath once more for four counts. This focused breathing can lower stress levels and mitigate feelings of anxiety or panic.

Engaging in rapid, intense physical activity like jumping jacks or push-ups can release endorphins, which counteract negative feelings and improve mood almost instantaneously.

Visualizing a calming or happy scene can provide a quick emotional reset. This technique engages the brain's imaginative faculties, creating a mental buffer against the encroachment of negative feelings.

The act of writing down your feelings can serve as a form of emotional catharsis, helping to clarify the underlying issues and potentially revealing patterns that contribute to negative emotional states. Over time, journaling can help you identify triggers and develop effective coping mechanisms.

For persistent negative feelings, CBT can be a highly effective long-term strategy. It involves identifying distorted thinking patterns and replacing them with more rational, balanced thoughts. This form of therapy can offer sustained relief from chronic emotional challenges.

Regular mindfulness meditation practice has been shown to reduce the recurrence of negative feelings by fostering greater emotional awareness and control. Over time, it can help rewire neural pathways associated with emotional regulation.

Learning to set and maintain healthy emotional boundaries can be a powerful long-term strategy for managing negative feelings. By clearly defining what is and isn't acceptable in your interactions with others, you're better equipped to protect your emotional well-being.

Incorporating these immediate and long-term strategies into your emotional regulation toolkit can significantly enhance your ability to manage negative feelings. Whether you're facing a sudden onslaught of emotional distress or grappling with chronic, recurring negativity, these techniques offer adaptable solutions designed to bring equilibrium and stability to your emotional landscape. By mastering these strategies, you empower yourself to navigate life's ups and downs with resilience, poise, and an enhanced sense of control.

As we've delved into the intricacies of feelings, emotions, and control, it becomes increasingly clear that learning plays a pivotal role in shaping our mental landscape. But why is the drive to learn so deeply ingrained in our neural circuitry? And how does this quest for knowledge influence our emotional well-being and cognitive flexibility?

The human brain is an information-gathering powerhouse designed to constantly scan the environment, absorb new data, and adapt accordingly. This is not a mere quirk of evolution but a survival imperative. Our ancestors, who were better at learning, had a competitive edge—they could adapt to changing environments, find food more efficiently, or evade predators more effectively.

The brain's built-in reward systems reflect this evolutionary bias towards learning. Dopamine, the neurotransmitter often associated with pleasure and reward, is released during the learning process, particularly when new information leads to successful outcomes. This dopamine release serves as a neural reinforcement, encouraging further learning endeavours.

The brain's plasticity—its ability to form new neural connections—also underscores the imperative of learning. Each new piece of information, skill acquired, or concept understood leads to the formation or strengthening of neural pathways, making the brain more versatile and adaptable.

Learning isn't just a cognitive exercise; it has profound implications for our emotional well-being and cognitive flexibility. The acquisition of new skills or knowledge can significantly boost self-esteem and contribute to a sense of purpose or achievement, enhancing emotional well-being. Moreover, the act of learning can serve as an effective coping mechanism during emotionally challenging times, offering a constructive diversion from negative thought patterns or feelings.

The more we learn, the more cognitive tools we have at our disposal to approach problems, make decisions, and even regulate our emotions. This cognitive flexibility is an often-overlooked benefit of learning. For instance, understanding the principles of emotional regulation or the neurobiology of stress can enhance your ability to manage your emotional states.

Learning about emotional intelligence, empathy, and effective communication can significantly improve interpersonal relationships. This emotional skill set, once learned, not only enhances social interactions but also contributes to emotional well-being by reducing conflict and fostering meaningful connections.

The imperative of learning is deeply embedded in our neural architecture, driven by evolutionary pressures and rewarded by neurochemical processes. Nevertheless, its benefits extend far beyond mere survival or cognitive expansion.

Learning enriches our emotional landscape, equips us with the tools for effective emotional regulation, and enhances cognitive flexibility, enabling us to navigate the complexities of modern life with greater ease and resilience. As we continue to explore the multifaceted aspects of brain function and emotional control, the role of learning emerges not merely as a peripheral theme but as a central, unifying concept that profoundly influences our capacity to live fulfilling emotionally balanced lives.

The quest for knowledge need not be a phase confined to formal education or early adulthood. Instead, the concept of lifelong learning advocates for an ongoing, voluntary pursuit of knowledge throughout one's life.

When engaged in lifelong learning, the mind remains agile and capable, constantly evolving to assimilate new information. This continual cognitive stimulation aids in problem-solving, as a well-exercised brain is more proficient in devising innovative solutions to complex challenges.

Lifelong learners can adapt more easily to new situations. Whether it's a career change, technological advancements, or shifts in social dynamics, a habit of consistent learning prepares you to navigate these changes with skill and ease.

The emotional payoff of being a lifelong learner is substantial. The consistent pursuit of knowledge engenders a sense of purpose and achievement, acting as a buffer against emotional setbacks. When invested in learning, disappointments and failures become less about personal inadequacy and more about opportunities for learning and growth, enhancing emotional resilience.

Lifelong learning isn't confined to academic or professional skills; it extends to emotional and social competencies. As you learn about emotional intelligence, conflict resolution, or even the art of effective communication, you become more skilled in managing your own emotions and understanding those of others, enriching both your emotional landscape and your social interactions.

Continual learning doesn't merely equip us with new skills or deepen our intellectual understanding; it also has a profound impact on how we perceive ourselves. The relationship between learning and self-perception is mutually reinforcing, forming a virtuous cycle that contributes to personal growth and well-being.

Each new skill mastered or concept understood contributes to a sense of competence and efficacy. This boosts self-esteem, reinforcing a positive self-image. The sense of achievement that accompanies the mastery of a new skill can be particularly empowering, elevating your perception of your own capabilities.

When you perceive yourself as competent and capable, you are more likely to seek new learning opportunities, perpetuating a cycle of positive self-perception and continued learning. This self-reinforcing loop not only enhances your skill set but also continually elevates your self-esteem, creating a sustained upward spiral in both competence and confidence.

As your self-perception improves, the intrinsic rewards of learning—such as the joy of discovery or the satisfaction of overcoming a challenge—become increasingly motivating, driving you to continue your learning journey.

In conclusion, the merits of being a lifelong learner extend far beyond the accumulation of knowledge or skills. Lifelong learning enriches your cognitive abilities, enhances your emotional well-being, and uplifts your self-perception. It's a holistic approach to personal development, one that cultivates a balanced, fulfilling life marked by continuous growth, emotional resilience, and a deep-seated sense of self-worth.

THOUGHT, FEELING, CONTROL AND LEARNING

THOUGHT and its MASTERY

As we continue our exploration into the multifaceted workings of the brain and its profound influence on our lives, we arrive at a juncture that many consider the epicentre of human experience—thoughts. These intricate patterns of mental activity are not only by-products of cerebral complexity but also the architects of our realities. Thoughts shape our perceptions, mould our actions, and ultimately, write the narratives of our lives. Understanding these intricacies will help us understand "Why My Brain Hates Me."

In this chapter, we will delve into the nature of thoughts, tracing their origins within the intricate circuitry of the brain and unfurling the vast impact they have on our well-being. From understanding what thoughts are to the practical applications of controlling them for self-improvement, this chapter aims to offer a comprehensive insight into the fascinating realm of thought.

To embark on this exploration, let's start by defining what thoughts actually are. At its most basic, thought is a mental construct the brain creates as it processes information. But to describe thoughts as mere data points would be an oversimplification of monumental proportions. Thoughts are a complex interplay of cognition, emotion, and intention, interwoven in a manner that defines the human experience.

Thoughts come in various forms and can be classified into different categories based on their nature and origin. Conscious thoughts are those we are fully aware of and can often control or manipulate. These are the thoughts we deliberately choose to dwell upon, such as solving a problem or planning an event. Subconscious thoughts, on the other hand, operate below the level of conscious awareness but still exert significant influence on our behaviours and feelings.

Involuntary thoughts are those that seem to 'pop' into our minds without any conscious effort, often triggered by external stimuli or emotional states. Lastly, intentional thoughts are cultivated deliberately to achieve specific outcomes, like invoking positive feelings or focusing on a task.

Each thought is a culmination of a series of complex neurobiological events. Neurons fire, neurotransmitters transmit signals, and neural networks come alive, all to form what we experience as a singular 'thought.' This complexity is compounded when we consider that thoughts seldom exist in isolation. They are part of intricate thought patterns, shaped by our beliefs, past experiences, and even our cultural backgrounds, interlinked in ways that can be both harmonious and contradictory.

As we turn our focus to the genesis of thoughts, we must venture into the realm of neurobiology, where the sparks of mental activity are ignited. Thoughts don't materialize out of nowhere; they emerge from intricate neurobiological processes that are influenced by a host of factors, both internal and external. In this section, we'll dissect the various elements that contribute to the birth of thoughts, offering a panoramic view of the complex interplay between brain function, environmental stimuli, and personal history.

The birthplace of thought resides in a complex network of neurons, neurotransmitters, and synaptic connections. The collective activity of these neural interactions forms the basis of thought.

The pre-frontal cortex, the frontal part of the brain located just behind the forehead, plays a significant role in generating conscious thoughts. It's responsible for executive functions like decision-making, planning, and rational thinking. Here, multiple streams of information from various parts of the brain converge to be integrated and processed, resulting in what we experience as coherent, logical thought.

"Imagine your brain as a bustling city, with neurons being the individual buildings and the roads between them as the synapses. Now, when one building "lights up" (which is like a neuron firing), it sends out a "message" to other buildings. This message is like a car travelling down the road, which, in biological terms, is a chemical signal. When the vehicle reaches another building, it has two main options: it can either tell that building to light up too or to stay dark. This series of buildings lighting up or remaining dark across the entire city is how you can think of thoughts forming in your brain.

So, you might wonder, where's the mayor's office in this brain city? Well, that would be the pre-frontal cortex, the section of the brain located right behind your forehead. This area acts like a control center where lots of different information from around the city comes in. It's like the mayor taking reports from all departments—transportation, utilities, public safety—and making a well-informed decision that affects the whole city. Similarly, your pre-frontal cortex takes information from different parts of your brain, puts it all together, and helps you make decisions, plan things, and think logically.

So, in essence, your thoughts come from a highly organized series of signals between buildings (neurons) in a city (your brain), coordinated by a very busy mayor's office (the pre-frontal cortex). This grand collaboration allows you to make sense of the world, plan your day, decide between options, and so much more."

Our external environment is a rich tapestry of stimuli that the brain continuously processes and it's a significant source of the material upon which thoughts are built. Whether it's the sights we see, the sounds we hear, or the people we interact with, our external environment provides a constant stream of data for our brain to evaluate, analyze, and respond to.

Thoughts are often shaped by the social norms, values, and cultural context we are exposed to. These external influences can affect how we think about ourselves, other people, and the world at large, subtly shaping our thought patterns in ways we may not always consciously recognize.

Just as external factors shape our thoughts, so too do our internal emotional states and past experiences. Our thoughts are often tinged, if not outright shaped, by the emotions we are feeling at any given time. For example, when we're anxious, our thoughts often spiral toward worst-case scenarios, while feelings of happiness can make even challenging situations seem more manageable.

Our history plays an indelible role in shaping our thoughts. Past experiences, especially emotionally charged ones, can create mental frameworks or schemas that influence how we interpret new information. These schemas act like cognitive filters, colouring our thoughts in ways that can be either helpful or detrimental, depending on the nature of the experiences that shaped them.

In essence, thoughts are not merely the by-products of isolated neurological activity but are shaped by a dynamic interplay of neurobiological processes, external influences, and personal history. Understanding these origins adds another layer to our ability to master our thoughts, equipping us with the knowledge to navigate the labyrinthine corridors of our minds with greater clarity and purpose.

As we build upon our understanding of what thoughts are and where they come from, the question that naturally follows is whether we can influence the quality of our thoughts. The answer is a resounding yes. The brain's plasticity enables us to reshape our thought patterns, offering us the potential to transition from negative to positive thinking. In this section, we'll outline effective methods for identifying negative thought patterns, explore actionable strategies for converting negativity into positivity, and discuss cognitive techniques for maintaining a positive mindset over the long term.

Recognizing negative thought patterns is the first critical step toward shifting to a more positive mindset. Being mindful of the language we use in our inner monologue can be revealing. Words like "never," "can't," or "should" often signify limiting beliefs.

Pay attention to your 'inner critic' that magnifies flaws, berates failures, or forecasts doom. By becoming aware of when this critic is active, you can challenge its assertions and begin the process of shifting toward more constructive thought patterns.

Maintaining a thought journal can be an effective way to track recurring negative thoughts. By documenting your thoughts, you can better understand their triggers and patterns, thereby making it easier to address them.

Once you've identified negative thought patterns, the next step is to replace them with positive alternatives. This involves consciously recognizing a negative thought and immediately replacing it with a positive one. For example, changing "I'll never be able to do this" to "I'll do the best I can and learn from the experience" can have a profound impact on your emotional state.

Another approach is to challenge the validity of your negative thoughts. Ask yourself questions like, "Is this thought based on facts? Is it a rational thought? What evidence do I have to support it?" More often than not, you'll find that your negative thoughts are based on unfounded fears or distortions.

While individual strategies can be effective in the short term, achieving long-term positivity requires a more systemic approach. Cognitive Behavioral Therapy is a proven method for long-term thought alteration. It involves identifying distorted thought patterns and replacing them with rational ones, thereby enabling sustained positive thinking.

Mindfulness techniques, often reinforced through meditation, can help you become more aware of your thoughts, making it easier to identify and alter negative patterns as they arise.

The transition from negative to positive thinking is not merely wishful thinking; it's a feasible goal that's backed by cognitive science. By employing a combination of identification strategies and thought alteration techniques, you can shift the gears of your mind towards a more positive, constructive outlook. This doesn't just make you feel better; it fundamentally enhances your ability to navigate life's challenges and opportunities, enriching your overall quality of life.

As we transition from understanding the mechanics of thought to the practical aspects of mastering it, the focus naturally shifts to the benefits that come with positive thinking. Beyond the immediate emotional uplift, maintaining a positive mindset has profound implications for various aspects of our lives. In this section, we'll explore how positive thinking not only contributes to emotional well-being but also manifests in tangible ways across different life domains, including health, relationships, and career.

The influence of positive thinking on emotional well-being is both immediate and enduring. A positive mindset acts as a buffer during stressful situations, allowing for better emotional regulation. Over time, this emotional resilience becomes ingrained, making it easier to navigate future challenges.

Positive thinking helps maintain an emotional equilibrium, reducing the intensity and duration of negative emotional states like anger, anxiety, or sadness. This leads to a more balanced emotional life, which in turn contributes to better mental health.

The positive impact of optimistic thinking extends well beyond emotional landscapes into real-world outcomes. Studies have shown that positive thinking can boost the immune system, improve cardiovascular health, and even contribute to longer life expectancy. A positive outlook can also enhance your ability to recover from illnesses and surgeries more quickly.

In relationships, a positive attitude can improve communication, increase empathy, and strengthen bonds. People are naturally attracted to positivity, which can lead to more meaningful and rewarding interpersonal interactions.

In the professional realm, a positive mindset is often linked to higher levels of productivity, better problem-solving abilities, and more remarkable career advancement. Employers value individuals who bring positivity to the workplace, which usually correlates with improved teamwork and leadership skills.

The concept of affirmations, or positive self-talk, is grounded in the understanding that our thoughts shape our reality. We need to define what affirmations are, explore the psychological foundations of this practice, and offer practical guidelines for incorporating affirmations into your daily life effectively to have a better understanding.

Affirmations are positive statements that are used to challenge and undermine negative beliefs or reinforce positive ones. The psychology behind affirmations is rooted in self-efficacy and cognitive dissonance theories. Regularly affirming positive beliefs about oneself creates a

THOUGHT AND ITS MASTERY

cognitive dissonance—or tension—between one's affirmations and any existing negative beliefs. This tension often resolves in favour of positive beliefs, leading to changes in attitude, behaviour, and even external circumstances.

Affirmations serve as a form of cognitive reinforcement, strengthening neural pathways that support positive beliefs. This makes it easier to default to a positive mindset over time, even when faced with challenging situations.

Harnessing the power of affirmations involves more than simply reciting positive statements. To maximize their effectiveness, it's important to adhere to specific guidelines that make these statements resonate more deeply with your subconscious mind. Below, we delve into these guidelines in greater detail, offering examples for each to illustrate how you can craft affirmations that genuinely contribute to a more positive mindset.

The believability of your affirmation is crucial for its effectiveness. If the statement doesn't resonate with you, your subconscious mind will reject it, rendering the exercise futile.

Example: Instead of saying, "I am the best at everything I do," which may feel too broad or unrealistic, try "I am becoming more skilled in my work every day." This statement is both positive and grounded in a realistic framework of continual improvement.

The more specific your affirmation is, the easier it is to envision achieving it, making it more likely that you will. Vague affirmations can be hard to measure and, therefore, harder to believe.

Example: Instead of saying, "I am loved," specify the source or nature of that love: "I am cherished by my family and friends."

Actionable affirmations include a clear action step or a behavioural change that you can make to move toward the goal represented by the affirmation. This makes your affirmation a call to action, not just a static statement.

Example: Instead of saying, "I am financially stable," try, "I am taking steps to improve my financial stability by saving 10% of my income."

Affirmations are most effective when phrased in the present tense. This creates a sense of immediacy and urgency, making it easier to visualize the affirmation as a current reality.

Example: Rather than saying, "I will be more confident," say, "I am building my confidence daily."

For affirmations to make a meaningful impact, they must be repeated consistently. Set aside time each day to consciously focus on your affirmations. Write them down, say them out loud, or even record them and listen to them regularly.

Example: Set reminders on your phone or post notes around your living space that display your affirmations, ensuring you encounter them multiple times throughout the day.

Choose affirmations that evoke a positive emotional response when you say them. The emotional charge enhances the affirmation's impact, making it more likely to stick.

Example: If you are seeking peace, an affirmation like "I am embracing calmness in every moment" should evoke feelings of tranquillity and peace.

As we've journeyed through the complexities of thought—from its origins to its potential for transformation—we can reach the ultimate goal of mastering the mind for self-improvement. The benefits of thought regulation extend far beyond the immediate moment; they offer a long-lasting impact that pervades multiple facets of life.

THOUGHT AND ITS MASTERY

The long-term advantages of gaining control over our thoughts, along with specific examples that illustrate the profound effects on emotional resilience, cognitive function, and overall life satisfaction, can be beneficial to understanding ourselves and our thinking.

The act of controlling your thoughts is akin to steering a ship; the better you can navigate, the smoother your journey through life. Over the long term, thought regulation contributes to mental stability, emotional well-being, and heightened self-awareness.

Regularly practicing thought control helps declutter the mind, leading to increased mental clarity and focus. This, in turn, enables better decision-making and problem-solving skills, as your mental resources are not entangled in negative thought spirals.

Learning to regulate your thoughts also means gaining better control over your emotions. You become less susceptible to mood swings and emotional upheavals, leading to more stable relationships and a more balanced life.

To offer a practical perspective, let's consider specific instances where thought control can bring about significant improvements in various aspects of life.

Imagine facing a challenging work project. Without thought control, it's easy to spiral into anxiety and self-doubt. However, with the ability to regulate your thoughts, you can redirect your focus towards constructive problem-solving and maintain emotional composure, demonstrating emotional resilience.

Consider the cognitive benefits during educational pursuits. If you can control distracting or defeatist thoughts during study sessions, your concentration and information retention rates improve significantly, enhancing your overall academic performance.

Thought control has a multiplier effect on life satisfaction. For instance, better emotional regulation means more fulfilling relationships.

Improved focus and mental clarity lead to professional achievements. These elements come together to elevate your overall sense of well-being and life satisfaction.

In summary, mastering the art of thought control is not just an exercise in mental discipline; it's a transformative practice that enriches your life in multifaceted ways. From honing emotional resilience to optimizing cognitive functions and enhancing life satisfaction, the benefits are as profound as they are pervasive. This mastery is not an endpoint but an ongoing process, a continual refinement that offers ever-deepening layers of self-awareness and personal growth.

THOUGHT AND ITS MASTERY

THE *inner* BATTLEFIELD

As we go deeper into the labyrinth of the human mind, we encounter a terrain that, while familiar, is often fraught with challenges—mental struggles that manifest as battles within our minds. These internal conflicts can range from fleeting moments of indecision to prolonged periods of anxiety or self-doubt and a better understanding of "Why My Brain Hates Me." Far from being abstract mental exercises, these internal battles have concrete impacts on our emotional well-being, decision-making abilities, and overall quality of life. Acknowledging and addressing these mental struggles is not just crucial for our psychological health but vital for achieving a fulfilling, well-balanced life.

The battlefield of the mind is a complex arena, riddled with diverse challenges that require nuanced strategies for overcoming them. To lay the groundwork for such a strategy, we first need to identify the types of mental battles that commonly occur to understand "Why My Brain Hates Me,"

Before we can conquer the enemy, we must know what—or who—we're up against. Mental struggles are as varied as they are common. Here are a few types that most people encounter at some point.

THE INNER BATTLEFIELD

Anxiety is a ubiquitous mental struggle that often manifests in various forms—be it social anxiety that makes interpersonal interactions nerve-wracking, performance anxiety that cripples your ability in high-stakes situations, or generalized anxiety disorder that casts a shadow over your everyday life.

Self-doubt is the nagging voice of self-doubt that can be an insidious enemy. It questions your capabilities, undermines your confidence, and stymies your growth. Whether doubting your worth in relationships or your competence in professional settings, self-doubt is a versatile foe that can appear in multiple arenas of life.

A less conspicuous but equally debilitating form of mental struggle is indecision. The inability to make clear decisions not only stalls progress but also fosters a breeding ground for anxiety and regret. Chronic indecision can be paralyzing, whether choosing a career path, making a significant life change, or deciding what to have for dinner.

One of the most pervasive forms of mental struggle is negative self-talk. This internal monologue consists of a constant stream of self-criticism, often belittling your achievements and exaggerating your shortcomings. This form of mental strife can have a cascading effect on your emotional health, exacerbating stress and contributing to states of anxiety and depression.

Procrastination is another formidable adversary in the mental realm. While it may initially seem harmless or even justified, chronic procrastination can significantly derail your personal and professional aspirations. It often acts as a buffer against the fear of failure or judgment, leading to a vicious cycle where the fear of not completing a task to perfection becomes a self-fulfilling prophecy, causing further delays and inefficiencies.

Related to both procrastination and self-doubt, perfectionism is a double-edged sword. On the one hand, it drives you to produce high-quality work; on the other, it can become an oppressive force that prevents you from completing tasks or taking risks for fear of making mistakes. The pursuit of unattainable standards can lead to a constant state of dissatisfaction and unnecessary stress.

Imposter Syndrome is a form of mental battle often found among high-achieving individuals who, despite their accomplishments, feel like frauds who could be exposed at any moment. This persistent belief that you've only succeeded due to luck rather than competence can severely limit your professional growth and personal development.

While not as immediate or tangible as other forms of mental struggles, existential angst deals with the more significant questions about meaning, purpose, and existence. Though typically less urgent, these concerns can create a pervasive sense of unease and dissatisfaction, affecting your outlook on life and your mental well-being in profound ways.

Rumination involves dwelling on past events or worrying about future ones, effectively trapping you in a cycle of unproductive thought. Whether it's replaying an embarrassing moment from five years ago or worrying about a future event, rumination can take a significant toll on your mental health, leading to increased levels of anxiety and depression.

With the advent of social media, the tendency to compare oneself to others has reached unprecedented levels. This constant comparison can lead to feelings of inadequacy, jealousy, and low self-esteem, further intensifying other forms of mental struggle like self-doubt and negative self-talk.

Each of these types of mental battles comes with its own set of challenges and nuances, requiring tailored approaches for effective management. Understanding the nature of these battles is the first step toward devising strategies to combat them. For example, cognitive-behavioural techniques can be highly effective for tackling negative self-talk, while mindfulness practices may offer significant relief from anxiety and rumination. Goal setting and time management strategies can be particularly useful for combatting procrastination. In contrast, professional therapy may be necessary for addressing more deep-seated issues like imposter syndrome or existential angst.

Importantly, these mental struggles are not isolated phenomena; they often coexist and interact in complex ways. For instance, procrastination may be a symptom of underlying perfectionism, which may be fueled by self-doubt. This interconnection means that addressing one area can often lead to improvements in another, creating a ripple effect of positive change.

The mental landscape is a complex and often challenging environment, fraught with various forms of internal strife. Yet, it's precisely this complexity that offers multiple avenues for growth and self-improvement. By identifying these common mental battles, understanding their unique characteristics, and implementing targeted strategies to address them, you set the stage for a more fulfilling, emotionally balanced life.

Understanding the landscape of mental struggles is incomplete without delving into the root causes that give rise to these internal battles. These underlying factors often operate in the background, subtly influencing our thoughts and emotions in ways that make us more susceptible to mental struggles. To dissect the root causes, it is helpful to consider them in three broad categories: Psychological factors, emotional factors, and situational factors.

When discussing the root causes of mental struggles, the role of psychological factors is both profound and pervasive. These factors often serve as the bedrock upon which our mental landscape is built, influencing our susceptibility to various types of mental struggles. The psychological factors can be broadly categorized into belief systems, cognitive biases, and mental habits, each having its unique impact on our mental well-being.

Our belief systems are a complex web of assumptions, values, and convictions that shape how we interpret the world around us. These beliefs are not just individual notions but are deeply rooted in our cultural background, family upbringing, and formative experiences. For instance, if you were raised in a family where academic success was highly valued, failing an exam could trigger intense anxiety or depressive thoughts far beyond the objective importance of that single test. Your belief system has shaped your perception of success and failure, and this perception influences your emotional response to events.

Cognitive biases are systematic patterns of deviation from rational thinking, affecting our judgments and decisions. One of the most impactful cognitive biases in the context of mental struggles is the negativity bias, which predisposes us to pay more attention to negative information or experiences. This bias can skew our perspective, making us focus excessively on our shortcomings, failures, or the risks we face, thereby fueling anxiety, depression, or other forms of mental unrest. Another bias that can contribute to mental struggles is confirmation bias, where we seek out information that confirms our pre-existing beliefs or fears, ignoring evidence to the contrary. This can create a self-perpetuating cycle of negative thinking.

Mental habits, such as rumination or catastrophizing, can also significantly contribute to mental struggles. Rumination involves repeatedly going over a thought or a problem without completion, amplifying the emotional intensity of the thought and making it more challenging to find a solution or achieve emotional closure. Catastrophizing involves imagining the worst possible outcome in any given situation, thereby increasing stress and anxiety levels exponentially.

Understanding these psychological factors in detail can provide a roadmap for navigating mental struggles more effectively. By becoming aware of the belief systems that shape our perceptions, recognizing the cognitive biases that skew our thinking, and identifying the mental habits

THE INNER BATTLEFIELD

that perpetuate our struggles, we are better equipped to take proactive steps. This can involve cognitive behavioural therapy to reframe negative thought patterns, mindfulness techniques to break the cycle of rumination, or simply seeking professional guidance to dissect and alter maladaptive belief systems. In doing so, we gain more than just insight; we gain the tools to build a more resilient mind.

The emotional landscape within us is a complex terrain moulded by a lifetime of experiences, relationships, and internal dialogues. It acts as both the foundation and the trigger for many of our mental struggles, intricately linked to how we perceive and interact with the world. One cannot discuss mental struggles in depth without giving due consideration to the role of emotional factors.

Our emotional history, for example, is a significant player in the shaping of our mental fabric. Events from our past, both large and small, create a sort of emotional fingerprint that influences our current emotional responses. These could range from significant traumas like loss or abuse to subtler emotional experiences such as neglect or humiliation. The echoes of these past emotional experiences often resurface when we encounter situations that serve as reminders, catalyzing current mental struggles.

Not only do past experiences influence our emotional state, but so does our current emotional well-being. Situations or states that trigger stress, anxiety, or even hormonal changes can heighten our emotional responses, making us more susceptible to mental struggles. For instance, ongoing stress can lower our emotional resilience, making us more reactive and less capable of effectively managing mental challenges.

Moreover, emotional regulation—or the lack thereof—can directly contribute to the mental struggles we face. Individuals who have not learned effective emotional regulation techniques are often at a higher risk for a range of mental struggles, from anxiety and depression to more complex emotional disorders. They might find themselves trapped in a cycle where emotional impulsivity feeds into mental struggles, which in turn exacerbate their emotional instability.

Even transient emotional states can have an outsized impact. For example, a temporary bout of loneliness can make one more susceptible to negative self-talk, which in turn can instigate or aggravate mental struggles. The same applies to positive transient states; a moment of happiness or contentment can sometimes be enough to halt or reduce mental struggles temporarily, proving the intertwined relationship between our emotional state and mental struggles.

The recognition and understanding of these emotional factors are instrumental in addressing mental struggles effectively. By identifying the emotional triggers and patterns that contribute to our mental state, we can develop more targeted strategies for emotional regulation. This will not only help in alleviating current mental struggles but also arm us with the emotional intelligence needed to navigate future challenges more adeptly.

To truly understand the intricate dynamics that contribute to mental struggles, it's crucial to examine the situational factors that often serve as the triggering events or aggravating conditions. While internal emotional and psychological factors set the stage, situational factors often act as the catalysts that bring latent struggles to the forefront.

Situational factors encompass a range of external circumstances that can dramatically impact our mental well-being. These can include high-stress environments such as workplaces where excessive demands and low support are the norm. In such settings, the relentless pressure can erode mental resilience, making individuals more susceptible to anxiety, depression, and other forms of mental struggles.

Another common situational factor is the state of our interpersonal relationships. Strained relationships, whether with family, friends, or partners, can be emotionally draining and mentally taxing. Conflicts, misunderstandings, or the absence of emotional support can trigger or

THE INNER BATTLEFIELD

exacerbate existing mental struggles, adding an additional layer of complexity to our emotional landscape.

Significant life changes, too, fall under the umbrella of situational factors. Events like moving to a new city, starting a new job, or experiencing a breakup or divorce can be profoundly disorienting. The uncertainty and upheaval that accompany these changes can serve as a breeding ground for mental struggles. Even positive life changes, like getting married or landing a dream job, can introduce a level of stress and expectation that may aggravate existing mental conditions.

Financial strain is another situational factor that often goes unnoticed. The stress associated with financial instability can be a potent trigger for mental struggles. The constant worry about making ends meet can lead to sleep issues, anxiety disorders, and even depressive states.

It's also worth mentioning that situational factors can sometimes be acute, short-term events that have long-lasting impacts. A traumatic event, such as an accident or the sudden loss of a loved one, can have immediate and enduring effects on mental health.

In summary, situational factors play a pivotal role in shaping our mental state. They act as triggers or amplifiers that can either initiate or exacerbate mental struggles. Recognizing the impact of these situational elements is crucial for comprehensive mental health management. It allows us to understand the full scope of our mental struggles, thereby equipping us with the insight needed to navigate them more effectively.

Understanding the root causes of our mental struggles involves a complex interplay of psychological, emotional, and situational factors. Acknowledging and addressing these root causes is the first step in effective management and eventual resolution of these struggles. It provides a solid foundation upon which to build coping strategies, seek appropriate interventions, and foster a more harmonious relationship with our minds.

Conquering the mental battles we face involves a combination of strategies tailored to the specific nature and underlying causes of each struggle.

In summary, mental struggles are an inevitable part of the human experience, but they don't have to define us. By identifying the types of mental battles we face, understanding their root causes, and employing effective strategies to combat them, we can regain control of our inner landscape. This chapter serves as a guide to navigating the complex terrain of the mind, equipping you with the tools and insights to emerge victorious in your own personal inner battles.

THE INNER BATTLEFIELD

SELF-CONCEPT

As we move deeper into the intricacies of "Why My Brain Hates Me," we arrive at a critical juncture—the psychology of self. Understanding how we perceive ourselves is not just an exercise in self-exploration; it holds the key to our mental well-being. Our self-concept, which encompasses our level of confidence, self-esteem, and the insecurities we harbour, acts as a lens through which we view the world. It shapes our interactions, influences our mental health, and ultimately determines our level of life satisfaction. Thus, understanding this intricate web of self-perception is crucial for mental well-being and the mastery of the mind we seek.

Navigating the terrain of the self inevitably leads us to confront the darker areas of insecurity and low self-esteem. These aspects of our self-concept, often neglected or misunderstood, have origins that are both complex and deeply rooted.

Feelings of insecurity and low self-esteem are often traced back to our early life experiences. The environment in which we were raised, the attitudes of our caregivers, and our early social experiences all contribute to the foundation upon which our self-concept is built. For instance, a child who was constantly criticized may grow into an adult plagued by insecurity.

SELF-CONCEPT

Society plays a significant role in shaping our self-concept, often in ways that foster insecurity and low self-esteem. Social norms, media portrayals, and even language can subtly instill feelings of inadequacy. For example, societal standards of beauty or success can make individuals feel insufficient or unworthy if they don't measure up.

Mental health conditions such as depression or anxiety disorders can also contribute to feelings of insecurity and low self-esteem. These psychological states often create a negative feedback loop, where the mental condition exacerbates feelings of low self-worth, which in turn worsens the condition.

Specific incidents or periods of intense stress and trauma can significantly impact our self-concept. Whether it's a failed relationship, job loss, or public humiliation, such events can instill deep-seated insecurities and significantly lower self-esteem.

By identifying and understanding the origins of our insecurities and low self-esteem, we lay the groundwork for rebuilding a healthier, more positive self-concept. It provides us with the context we need to challenge these negative beliefs about ourselves, thereby opening the door for transformation and growth. This is not merely an act of self-improvement but a fundamental necessity for enhancing our mental well-being and overall quality of life.

In the quest for mental well-being, understanding the origins of insecurity and low self-esteem is only half the battle. The next, and perhaps most crucial, step involves rebuilding a more robust and positive sense of self. To move from understanding to action, let's delve into a step-by-step guide that offers actionable strategies for boosting self-confidence and self-esteem.

The first step in any transformational journey is self-awareness. Identifying your strengths and weaknesses, as well as understanding your insecurities and what triggers low self-esteem, gives you the context you need for change.

Example One: Keep a journal documenting moments when you feel particularly insecure or confident. Over time, look for patterns or common triggers.

Confidence is built on a series of small victories. Setting achievable goals that you can reach in the short term provides the momentum necessary for long-term change.

Example Two: Break down larger goals into smaller, manageable tasks. Celebrate each accomplishment, however minor it may seem.

It's challenging to grow in a vacuum. Constructive feedback from trusted friends, family, or mentors can offer invaluable perspectives you may not have considered.

Example Three: Ask for feedback after completing a task or reaching a milestone. Use this information for continual self-improvement.

Our internal dialogue plays a significant role in shaping our self-concept. Challenging and changing negative self-talk can have a profound impact on your level of self-confidence.

Example Four: Whenever you catch yourself engaging in negative self-talk, counter it with evidence that supports a more positive viewpoint.

One of the most effective ways to boost self-confidence is to become more competent. Whether it's a professional skill or a personal hobby, mastery breeds confidence.

Example Five: Choose a skill you've always wanted to learn and dedicate time to mastering it. Monitor your progress and celebrate your improvements.

The people you surround yourself with have a significant impact on your self-esteem. Engaging in positive relationships can serve as a buffer against insecurity and low self-esteem.

Example Six: Evaluate your current relationships and consider distancing yourself from individuals who consistently bring you down. Seek out and nurture relationships with those who uplift you.

Last but not least, be kind to yourself. Self-compassion provides the emotional resilience needed to face setbacks and failures, which are inevitable on any transformative journey.

Example Seven: Develop a self-compassion mantra that you can turn to in challenging times. It could be as simple as "I am doing my best, and that is enough."

Building self-confidence is a layered and ongoing process. By following these actionable steps, you not only set the stage for enhancing your self-esteem but also create a ripple effect that positively influences your overall mental well-being. The objective is not to attain some elusive state of perfection but to engage in continuous self-improvement that elevates your quality of life.

While personal commitment and internal strategies are invaluable for boosting self-confidence and self-esteem, external tools and resources can provide additional support and guidance. Here, we explore evidence-based tools that have been scientifically proven to aid in self-improvement.

Cognitive Behavioural Therapy is a widely used psychological treatment that has been empirically proven to improve various mental health conditions, including issues related to low self-esteem and confidence. Many online platforms and apps offer CBT exercises. However, for a more personalized approach, consider consulting a licensed therapist.

Mindfulness and Meditation Apps improve mental well-being, including self-esteem. Apps like Headspace and Calm offer guided mindfulness sessions that can be easily incorporated into your daily routine.

Self-Help Books, though not a substitute for professional advice, self-help books based on psychological research can offer valuable insights into improving self-confidence and self-esteem.

Online Courses and Webinars offer courses specifically geared towards improving self-concept. The journey of self-improvement is not a straight path but a winding road with ups and downs. It's crucial to have markers along the way to gauge your progress and adjust your strategies as needed.

Regularly evaluate your levels of self-confidence and self-esteem through self-assessment questionnaires. Many validated scales are available for this purpose. Utilize assessments like the Rosenberg Self-Esteem Scale periodically to track your progress.

Documenting your experiences, feelings, and milestones in a journal can provide valuable insights into your journey. It can also serve as a record to reflect on how far you've come. Revisit your journal entries at the end of each month to identify areas of improvement and set new goals for the coming month.

As you make progress, the people around you will likely notice changes in your behaviour, attitude, and interactions. Use this external feedback as an additional metric for gauging your improvement. Periodically ask trusted individuals for feedback on changes they've noticed in your confidence or general demeanour.

Achieving goals, whether big or small, serves as concrete evidence of your growing self-confidence and improved self-esteem. Keep a record of your accomplishments and celebrate these milestones, using them as a source of motivation to continue on your path.

In conclusion, the road to improved self-concept is a multi-faceted endeavour that benefits from a blend of internal efforts and external resources. By employing evidence-based tools, staying committed to actionable steps, and measuring your progress through reliable metrics,

SELF-CONCEPT

you can navigate the intricacies of self-improvement with greater confidence and efficacy. The ultimate aim is not merely to improve your self-concept but to foster a healthier, more fulfilling life.

NEGATIVE THOUGHTS

As we continue to explore the landscape of mental well-being, we encounter one of the most pervasive obstacles to a fulfilling life—negative thoughts. These insidious patterns of thinking, often dismissed or overlooked, hold immense sway over our emotional state, decision-making abilities, and overall mental health. Understanding these insidious patterns will help us understand "Why My Brain Hates Me."

Far from being inconsequential inner murmurs, negative thoughts can become self-fulfilling prophecies that reinforce cycles of emotional distress, anxiety, and even depression. Therefore, understanding and combating negative thoughts is not just an exercise in mental hygiene; it's a prerequisite for achieving optimal mental health and quality of life.

Understanding the origins of negative thinking is essential for gaining control over this debilitating mental habit. The roots of negative thinking are often deeply embedded in a variety of factors, each contributing its own weight to the overarching issue.

One significant contributor to negative thinking is our brain's natural cognitive biases. The negativity bias is particularly influential, as it predisposes us to pay greater attention to negative information. This bias

NEGATIVE THOUGHTS

dates back to our evolutionary past when focusing on potential dangers was a matter of survival. In the modern world, however, this bias often works against us, compelling us to dwell on threats that may be neither imminent nor significant, thus amplifying our anxieties and fears.

Environmental influences are another key determinant of negative thought patterns. The settings in which we live, work, and socialize can significantly influence our mindset. For example, a toxic work environment characterized by constant criticism can make us more prone to seeing the world through a negative lens. Similarly, family dynamics or social circles that are fraught with negativity can have a substantial impact, conditioning us to adopt pessimistic thought patterns over time.

Emotional states like depression, anxiety, or heightened stress levels can also accentuate negative thinking. These conditions often create a feedback loop where negative thoughts perpetuate emotional distress, which in turn fuels more negative thinking. The vicious cycle can be particularly difficult to break, especially without professional intervention or effective coping mechanisms.

Our past experiences also play a crucial role in shaping our thought patterns. Emotional events from our past, particularly those that were traumatic or had a lasting impact, can set the stage for persistent negative thinking. For instance, if someone has experienced failure in a significant aspect of life, such as a career or relationship, the memory of that failure can lead to recurring thoughts that undermine self-esteem and foster negativity.

Understanding these origins is not just an academic exercise; it's a vital part of the path toward mental wellness. Each contributing factor—be it cognitive biases, environmental settings, emotional conditions, or past experiences—offers a potential point for intervention. By recognizing and understanding these origins, we can devise more effective strategies to counteract negative thinking. This enables us to break the self-perpetuating cycle of negativity, equipping us with the tools we need to improve our emotional well-being and overall quality of life.

Transforming negative thought patterns into more positive ones isn't an overnight process; it requires ongoing effort, attention, and a variety of techniques tailored to individual needs. One effective approach is cognitive reframing. This isn't about sugar-coating reality but about shifting your perspective to see challenges as opportunities for growth rather than threats. For example, instead of drowning in the thought that you're not good at something, reframe it to acknowledge that you're not good at it yet, but you have the opportunity to improve with effort and practice.

Thought-stopping is another practical technique. It's as straightforward as it sounds: catch yourself when a negative thought starts to spiral and consciously choose to stop it. For some people, having a physical cue, like snapping a rubber band worn on the wrist, helps halt the thought and serves as a reminder to switch gears mentally. This abrupt stop allows you to redirect your focus to more constructive thoughts or actions.

Mindfulness and meditation are often hailed for their stress-reducing benefits, and they also offer substantial help in recognizing and altering negative thought patterns. These practices train you to be more aware of your thoughts and feelings, giving you the opportunity to choose how you react. It's like strengthening a mental muscle that allows you to catch negativity before it festers and spirals out of control.

Gratitude journaling is another useful tool in your arsenal. This practice forces you to focus on the positives in your life, no matter how small they may seem. The act of writing down these positives engrains them deeper into your consciousness, serving as a counterbalance to the natural human tendency to focus on the negative. Over time, this practice can shift your default perspective from one of scarcity or negativity to one of abundance and positivity.

NEGATIVE THOUGHTS

Remember, these techniques are not one-size-fits-all solutions. They can be tailored to fit your specific needs, and it might take some experimentation to find the combination that works best for you. The key is to be consistent and intentional in your efforts, and over time, you'll likely find that the scales have tipped in favour of a more positive and healthier thought pattern.

Sustaining a positive thought pattern is an ongoing process that requires continuous effort and monitoring. Regularly use validated psychological scales designed to measure thought patterns, such as the Automatic Thoughts Questionnaire. Example: Periodic assessments can offer objective metrics for evaluating the improvement or deterioration of your thought patterns.

A journal can be an excellent tool for tracking changes in your thought patterns over time. Example: Use your journal to note both negative and positive thoughts and analyze them at the end of each week to gauge your progress.

Sharing your journey with someone you trust can provide an external perspective and emotional support to keep you on track. Example: Regularly update your accountability partner on your progress and challenges and seek their feedback for additional insights.

Recognizing and celebrating progress, no matter how small, can act as a positive reinforcement, encouraging the continuity of healthy thought patterns. Example: Create milestones for your journey, and each time you reach one, celebrate in a way that brings you joy.

The genesis of negative thoughts can often be traced back to our formative years, where the environment we grow up in significantly influences our cognitive development. The words and actions of trusted figures, such as parents, teachers, and family members, wield considerable power in shaping our self-perceptions. For many, this is where the seeds of negative thinking are sown. When those who should be nurturing our growth instead belittle, abuse, or neglect us, they create a cognitive landscape fertile for the growth of self-doubt, self-loathing, and other forms of negative thought patterns.

In an ideal world, the family unit serves as a sanctuary that provides children with emotional security and a sense of self-worth. However, dysfunctional families, marked by abuse, neglect, or constant criticism, distort this sanctuary into a breeding ground for negative thought patterns. The child learns to view the world and themselves through a lens coloured by insecurity and inadequacy.

Similar patterns can emerge in educational settings. Teachers hold a position of authority and are often viewed as role models. Negative comments or unfair treatment from a teacher can have long-lasting effects on a child's self-esteem and confidence. The consequences are often more than just academic; they can extend to how a child views their capabilities and potential, shaping their self-view in a way that can endure into adulthood.

Traumatic events, such as physical or emotional abuse, further compound the issue. Trauma disrupts the victim's sense of safety and self, often leading to a distorted perception of self-worth and a heightened state of alertness for future threats, both real and imagined. The brain may start to anticipate negativity or danger as a coping mechanism, thereby generating pervasive negative thoughts.

Understanding the origins of negative thoughts is crucial for effective intervention and the development of healthier thought patterns. Mindfulness techniques can be particularly useful in identifying triggers and thought patterns as they occur. This heightened awareness enables the individual to challenge these thoughts, examine their validity, and replace them with healthier alternatives.

It's worth noting that while the influences of early life experiences and trusted figures are powerful, they don't have to dictate the course of one's life. With the right strategies and support, it's entirely possible to rewrite these internal scripts. The process of overcoming negative thoughts often involves unlearning deeply ingrained beliefs and relearning healthier ways of perceiving oneself and the world. It's not an easy journey, but it is one that holds the promise of greater emotional freedom, self-acceptance, and a far more prosperous, more fulfilling life.

In conclusion, negative thoughts are not simply random occurrences; they often have their roots in our formative years and are influenced by the people we trust and the experiences we undergo. However, recognizing these root causes empowers us to challenge these thoughts and change them with the right tools and support. By doing so, we're not just altering our thought patterns but fundamentally transforming our relationship with ourselves.

Transforming negative thoughts into positive ones is a nuanced and ongoing process. By employing targeted techniques, monitoring your progress through reliable methods, and remaining committed to continuous improvement, you can break free from the clutches of negativity. The ultimate goal is to cultivate a mindset that not only improves your mental health but also enriches the overall quality of your life.

REGRETS, FLAWS, *and* WEAKNESSES

As we continue to traverse the nuanced landscape of mental well-being, we come face-to-face with the complex spectrum of human emotions. Far from being binary states of happiness or sadness, human emotions encompass a wide array of feelings, including regrets, flaws, and weaknesses. These emotions, often considered negative or undesirable, are integral aspects of the human experience. They shape our decision-making, influence our relationships, and play a significant role in our overall mental well-being. The impact of these emotions is not to be underestimated; they can either serve as stepping stones for growth or become stumbling blocks that impede progress. Thus, a deeper understanding of these complex emotions is essential not just for intellectual curiosity but for fostering a more balanced and harmonious life. It helps us to understand why "Why My Brain Hates Me."

Regret is an emotion that nearly everyone encounters at some point, often more than once. It's an emotional response that occurs when we evaluate our actions and decisions, often with a sense of loss or disappointment. Though commonly associated with negative feelings, regret is actually a multi-layered emotional and cognitive experience that can hold valuable lessons for personal growth and future decision-making.

Regret involves a cognitive process of evaluating actions, or even inactions, against a backdrop of what could have been. It's an emotional feedback mechanism that helps us assess the difference between our actual path and a path we wish we had taken. This could range from minor everyday decisions like wishing we had taken a different route to avoid traffic to more impactful life choices such as career paths, relationships, or missed opportunities. The scale of these regrets can vary, but their presence is almost ubiquitous in human life.

At its core, regret involves a counterfactual thought process, where we mentally compare our current situation with potential alternatives. This mental comparison is the breeding ground for the emotional component of regret. When the alternative appears better than reality, the emotional weight of regret sets in. It's our brain's way of saying, "You could have avoided this negative outcome if you had chosen differently." And it is precisely this realization that can be both enlightening and debilitating.

Regret can have significant psychological repercussions. A life filled with regret can contribute to stress, anxiety, and depression. In extreme cases, it can lead to a debilitating sense of hopelessness, where individuals feel trapped by their past decisions. The weight of regret can also affect current decision-making processes, leading to indecisiveness or overly cautious behaviour. After all, a person continually dwelling on past mistakes may become too afraid to take risks or make any changes, leading to a stagnant life.

However, regret also holds transformative potential. When approached constructively, regret can serve as a catalyst for meaningful change. Instead of wallowing in the sorrow of what could have been, we can use regret to reassess our priorities, values, and decision-making strategies. Understanding the root causes of our regrets can offer insights into our core beliefs, desires, and fears. This self-awareness can be an invaluable tool for personal growth, enabling us to make better decisions that align with our long-term goals and values.

For instance, regret over a failed relationship can offer insights into the kind of partner we're seeking and the dynamics we want to avoid in the future. Regretting over a missed career opportunity can motivate us to be more proactive in seizing future opportunities or even prompt a career change. These are examples of how regret can serve as a feedback mechanism that guides future behaviour and decision-making.

One of the most constructive ways to deal with regret is through reframing it as a learning opportunity. This involves a cognitive shift from focusing on the negative outcome to extracting valuable lessons from the experience. Learning from regret can be a proactive way to improve future decision-making and mitigate the chances of experiencing similar regrets later in life. This transformative approach turns regret from a source of pain into a tool for personal growth and future satisfaction.

Moreover, it's crucial to understand that regret is a common human experience. You are not alone in feeling this way, and it's okay to seek support. Discussing your regrets openly with trusted friends, family, or mental health professionals can provide different perspectives and even solutions that you might not have considered. Sometimes, the act of verbalizing these feelings can in itself be a therapeutic experience, lightening the emotional load and providing a sense of relief.

In summary, regrets and mistakes are inevitable facets of the human experience. But they don't have to define us. By acknowledging their existence and understanding their root causes, we can choose to use them as catalysts for change and self-improvement. The choice between letting regret serve as a paralyzing force or a propellant for growth is entirely up to us. Through a balanced understanding and constructive

REGRETS, FLAWS, AND WEAKNESSES

approach to our regrets, we can channel them into making more informed decisions, leading to a life of greater satisfaction and fewer future regrets.

As we delve deeper into the multifaceted realm of human emotions, we encounter an often uncomfortable yet inescapable reality—our flaws and weaknesses. These traits, far from being mere chinks in our armour, form an integral part of our identity. Whether it's impatience, a propensity for procrastination, or a short temper, these so-called "negative" traits can have a significant impact on our mental well-being and interpersonal relationships. However, they also offer an opportunity for profound self-awareness and growth.

Society often promotes an ideal of perfection, making us more likely to hide or deny our flaws and weaknesses. This social conditioning leads to a state of internal conflict, where we feel compelled to portray a version of ourselves that aligns with these unrealistic standards. However, this denial doesn't erase these traits; it merely suppresses them, often leading to increased stress and diminished mental well-being.

The first step in coming to terms with your flaws and weaknesses is accepting that they exist. Acceptance doesn't mean resignation; instead, it's an acknowledgment that forms the foundation for constructive action. Without accepting a flaw or weakness, it's nearly impossible to take the steps needed to improve or mitigate its impact.

It's crucial to understand that many weaknesses are the flip side of strengths. For instance, a person who is overly critical may have strong attention to detail, while someone who is viewed as excessively emotional may possess deep empathy for others. By identifying the positive aspects of our negative traits, we can channel them more productively.

Harboring flaws and weaknesses doesn't make us flawed human beings; it makes us human, period. Practicing self-compassion involves treating ourselves with the same kindness and understanding that we would offer a loved one. By doing so, we can navigate the emotional turbulence that often accompanies the recognition of our flaws and weaknesses.

Coming to terms with flaws and weaknesses is not a one-time event but a continuous journey of self-discovery and growth. As we evolve, so do our weaknesses and strengths, and the key is to remain adaptive, using new insights for ongoing self-improvement.

Learning to accept and even embrace our flaws and weaknesses is a transformative experience, one that frees us from the shackles of societal expectations and self-imposed limitations. This acceptance doesn't just alleviate emotional burdens; it enriches our understanding of who we are, enhancing both our mental well-being and the quality of our interactions with others. Ultimately, our flaws and weaknesses can serve as profound avenues for personal growth, but only if we allow ourselves the freedom to acknowledge, accept, and learn from them.

Regarding personal development, the focus often leans toward skill acquisition, productivity, or physical well-being. While these dimensions are undoubtedly important, they can't fully capture the breadth and depth of human growth. Emotional and psychological growth, though less tangible, are foundational to overall well-being and success. This means addressing the good, the bad, and the ugly within us—our strengths as well as our flaws, weaknesses, and regrets. These aspects, often relegated to the shadows of our self-improvement efforts, can actually serve as fertile ground for substantial growth.

Mindfulness, a term frequently thrown around in wellness circles, is not just another trend; it's a crucial practice for emotional and psychological development. Its importance lies in its capacity for increasing self-awareness. Mindfulness practices such as focused breathing, meditation, or even mindful walking can help you become acutely aware of your emotional triggers, behavioural patterns, and recurring thought loops. By shedding light on these areas, mindfulness paves the way for meaningful change. It allows you to catch yourself before you spiral into negativity or react impulsively, offering you the choice to steer your actions and thoughts in a direction that serves you better.

In addition to mindfulness, goal-setting serves as another potent tool for psychological growth. The key here is to set specific, measurable, achievable, relevant, and time-bound (SMART) goals that target areas for emotional and psychological improvement. These could range from improving your emotional regulation and enhancing your relationship skills to reducing procrastination or negative self-talk. When you set clear, achievable goals, you provide yourself with a roadmap that not only outlines your destination but also marks the milestones along the way. This keeps you motivated and allows you to measure your progress, making the process of personal growth more tangible and rewarding.

Another effective strategy involves cognitive-behavioural techniques. These methods are designed to help you identify negative thought patterns that often serve as the underpinning of emotional struggles, behavioural issues, or interpersonal conflicts. Once these patterns are identified, the next step involves challenging and reshaping these thoughts into more realistic and constructive ones. This cognitive restructuring is akin to mental decluttering; it frees up emotional bandwidth and allows for more adaptive thinking and behaviour. By consistently practicing these techniques, you can dramatically improve your emotional well-being and psychological resilience.

Professional guidance through therapy or counselling can also offer invaluable insights into your emotional and psychological landscape. Therapists can provide personalized coping strategies, targeted exercises, and a non-judgmental space for you to explore your emotional complexities. Their expertise can offer you fresh perspectives and coping mechanisms that you might not have considered, thereby accelerating your journey toward emotional maturity and psychological well-being.

Now, let's shift our focus to the application of emotional and psychological growth in real-world settings, such as in your relationships or workplace. Enhanced self-awareness and emotional intelligence don't just improve your relationship with yourself; they also profoundly impact your interactions with others. When you understand your own weaknesses and triggers, you become better equipped to understand those of others, thereby fostering more empathetic and meaningful relationships. In professional settings, this translates to better team dynamics and leadership skills. Leaders who are aware of their own emotional triggers and behavioural patterns are better equipped to manage diverse teams, address conflicts effectively, and create a work environment that leverages individual strengths for collective benefit.

Lastly, one of the most profound benefits of emotional and psychological growth is the significant improvement in life satisfaction. When you learn to see your flaws, weaknesses, and regrets as opportunities for growth rather than as immutable shortcomings, you undergo a paradigm shift that affects all areas of your life. You start viewing challenges as opportunities to learn and grow rather than threats. This shift in perspective contributes to a more profound sense of contentment, fulfillment, and overall well-being.

In conclusion, the path to emotional and psychological growth involves a multifaceted approach that includes mindfulness practices, goal-setting, cognitive-behavioural techniques, and even professional counselling when needed. The fruits of these labours are manifold, improving not just your self-awareness but also your interpersonal relationships and life satisfaction. So, the next time you find yourself weighed down by your perceived flaws or past regrets, remember that these are not just obstacles to be overcome; they're actually opportunities for profound personal growth. By learning to navigate the complex terrain of your emotional and psychological landscape, you'll be better equipped to face life's challenges, build meaningful relationships, and lead a fulfilling, balanced life.

REGRETS, FLAWS, AND WEAKNESSES

MISTAKES *and* BAD HABITS

When we talk about the struggles we face with our own minds, we often focus on diagnosable conditions or psychological issues. However, everyday mistakes and bad habits also play a significant role in why we sometimes feel our brain is working against us. This chapter aims to shed light on how these less-discussed factors contribute to our internal battles and offers strategies for overcoming them.

When it comes to mistakes, it's almost as if we're programmed to view them as the enemy, as markers of failure or incompetence. But let's take a step back and consider their role in our lives from a broader perspective. Mistakes are, in many ways, the natural byproducts of living a life in which we dare to take risks, make choices, and venture into the unknown. They're an inseparable part of our learning journey, occurring when our actions don't align with our intentions or when unforeseen circumstances throw a wrench into our plans.

If you think about it, mistakes are almost like life's lab experiments. You try something out, but it doesn't produce the result you wanted, and you go back to the drawing board. Only this time, you're armed with additional data about what doesn't work. The issue arises when we don't treat mistakes as data or as opportunities for reflection and adjustment. Instead, we often allow them to become emotional burdens that feed into negative self-perception. We turn them into mental narratives that say, "I messed up; therefore, I am a mess."

The mental and emotional toll of mistakes can be profound, especially when we start using them as a lens through which we view our self-worth. This is particularly troublesome when a mistake is a one-time event, an outlier, but we treat it as if it's the defining pattern of our lives. One failed relationship, for instance, can lead to thoughts like "I'm unlovable" or "I'll always be alone," which not only distort our self-view but also influence our future actions and decisions in unhealthy ways.

But why do we magnify the impact of our mistakes to such an extent? Part of the reason lies in societal conditioning. From a young age, we're often taught to aim for perfection to seek approval and validation from others, be it parents, teachers, or peers. This sets the stage for a mindset that equates mistakes with personal failure.

Psychological factors also come into play. Cognitive biases such as the "spotlight effect," where we think all eyes are on us, make us overestimate how much our mistakes matter to others. There's also the negativity bias, where negative events have a more significant impact on our psychological state than neutral or positive events. These biases can make each mistake feel like a monumental event everyone notices and judges, amplifying our emotional reaction and deepening our sense of inadequacy or shame.

The irony is that everyone makes mistakes; it's one of the few things that all humans have in common. Yet, we often feel as if we're the only ones messing up. This distorted perception isolates us, adding a layer of loneliness to the emotional weight of our errors.

So, how do we shift our perspective? First, by recognizing that mistakes, in themselves, are value-neutral. They are events, occurrences, and moments in time that provide feedback. They are not character indictments. Second, practicing self-compassion, which involves treating ourselves with the same kindness and understanding we'd offer to a friend in a similar situation. Self-compassion allows us to confront our mistakes without fear, to learn from them, and to move forward without the baggage of self-judgment.

Another effective strategy is to externalize the mistake, to see it as an event separate from our identity. This can be as simple as saying, "I did a bad thing" instead of "I am bad." This externalization provides the emotional distance needed to analyze the mistake objectively, to see it as a problem to be solved rather than a stain on our character.

Ultimately, the way we handle mistakes shapes not only our self-perception but also our approach to life's challenges and opportunities. When we see mistakes as learning experiences, we become more resilient, adaptable, and better equipped to navigate the complexities and uncertainties of life. We become more willing to take calculated risks and step out of our comfort zones. After all, if a mistake is just another opportunity to learn, then what's there to fear?

The concept of bad habits can sometimes feel abstract, almost like a nebulous cloud that hovers over our daily lives, subtly influencing our choices, actions, and, ultimately, our mental well-being. Suppose we were to dissect this cloud, to look at its anatomy. In that case, we'd find it's not just a random congregation of mist but a collection of precisely formed droplets—each representing different elements that contribute to the formation and persistence of bad habits.

Our brain has a reward system that involves the release of dopamine, a neurotransmitter associated with pleasure and reinforcement. When we engage in a behaviour that triggers this release, it feels good, and naturally, we're inclined to do it again. Over time, the neural pathways that link the behaviour to the reward get strengthened, almost like a well-trodden path in a forest. Each time you follow that path, it becomes more deeply ingrained, making it easier to take the next time. This neural reinforcement is a double-edged sword. It's the mechanism through which we form good habits like exercise, but it's also the reason why bad habits are so difficult to break. The brain doesn't necessarily differentiate between good and bad; it just knows what brings it immediate pleasure.

MISTAKES AND BAD HABITS

Now, this is where emotional factors come into play. Often, bad habits are coping mechanisms for emotional voids or stressors. For example, emotional eating isn't really about the food; it's about the emotional comfort or stress relief that the act of eating provides. Similarly, procrastination isn't a reflection of one's inability to perform a task but rather a way to avoid the anxiety or fear associated with it. Understanding the emotional triggers that lead to a bad habit can provide significant insights into how to break it. If you can identify what you're really seeking—be it comfort, stress relief, or even boredom relief—you can look for healthier ways to achieve the same emotional outcome.

The environment is another contributing factor. Our surroundings can have a significant impact on our behaviour, often more than we realize. Whether it's a social environment that encourages excessive drinking or a home setting that makes it easy to lounge around and avoid exercise, our external circumstances play a role in sustaining bad habits. Changing your environment to make the bad habit more difficult to engage in can be a crucial step in breaking it. This could mean avoiding situations where you're tempted to indulge in the habit or even rearranging your living space to make the habit less accessible.

Societal norms and peer pressure are also part of this equation. We're social creatures, and the people around us influence our behaviour in profound ways. If you're in a community where a particular bad habit is normalized or even glorified, breaking free from it becomes much more challenging. In such cases, expanding your social circle to include people who share your goal of breaking the habit can offer much-needed support and accountability.

While it's easy to think of bad habits as individual failings, they're often systemic in nature. This means that breaking them isn't just about willpower; it requires a comprehensive approach that addresses the habit from multiple angles: neural, emotional, environmental, and social. As you start to pull apart the threads that make up the fabric of the bad habit, you'll find that it becomes less daunting, more understandable, and ultimately, more manageable. Once we demystify the anatomy of bad habits, we can better equip ourselves to dismantle them, replacing them with healthier behaviours that serve us well in our journey toward emotional and psychological growth.

It's important to recognize the relationship between mistakes and bad habits. Sometimes, mistakes are one-time events that serve as wake-up calls, forcing us to reevaluate our actions and decisions. Bad habits, on the other hand, are often the result of repeated mistakes. Understanding this interplay can help us break the cycle. For instance, a mistake can serve as a trigger for a bad habit. If you're trying to quit smoking, stress from making a mistake at work might tempt you to light up a cigarette. Recognizing this pattern is the first step toward breaking it.

Encountering mistakes and bad habits is inevitable. These aren't mere annoyances but signposts on the road to self-discovery and personal growth. Let's set aside the moral judgments often attached to these terms and consider them as part of a larger, more complex emotional and psychological landscape.

When it comes to acknowledging mistakes, a compassionate lens is crucial. Harsh self-criticism rarely produces constructive outcomes; instead, it often feeds a cycle of negative thinking and emotional distress. The goal isn't to dwell on mistakes but to understand their origins and implications. In doing so, a more straightforward path to rectification and future avoidance often emerges. This isn't about absolving oneself of responsibility; it's about understanding the context in which these mistakes were made.

Bad habits present a somewhat different challenge. Unlike mistakes, which can be isolated events, bad habits are patterns of behaviour that have often been reinforced over time. Addressing them means not just dealing with individual instances but tackling an entire behavioural framework. While it's tempting to focus on the habit itself, a more helpful approach might be to identify the triggers and emotional states that lead to these behaviours. Is it stress? Boredom? Emotional discomfort? By identifying these triggers, strategies can be developed to cope with these feelings in a more constructive manner.

Goal-setting is often touted as a universal solution, but its effectiveness can be profoundly impacted by the specificity and realism of these goals. Rather than vague objectives like 'be better,' concrete, achievable targets provide both a roadmap and a measure of progress. Employing the SMART framework—Specific, Measurable, Achievable, Relevant, and Time-bound—even if not explicitly named, can offer a structured approach to what can often be a nebulous problem.

Professional help, while not always necessary, can provide invaluable assistance, particularly for more ingrained or destructive habits. Therapists and counsellors can offer insights and coping strategies that might not be immediately obvious. They can also provide that external accountability that friends and family might not be equipped to offer for all their good intentions.

Support networks, be they friends, family, or support groups, offer both emotional support and practical advice. Sometimes, it takes an external perspective to see things clearly, and there's often as much to learn from others' mistakes and bad habits as there is from one's own. The journey to overcoming these challenges is often long and filled with setbacks. A strong support network can provide the emotional resilience required to continue, even when it seems easier just to revert to old behaviours.

However, it's crucial to remember that setbacks are not the same as failures. The road to improvement is rarely a straight one; there will be detours and bumps along the way. The key is resilience and the ability to adapt strategies as needed. What works in one situation may not in another, and it's this flexibility that often proves to be the most valuable asset in overcoming mistakes and bad habits.

Monitoring progress can be motivating and enlightening, shedding light on successes and improvement areas. Even small victories are worth celebrating, as they serve as proof of concept that change is possible and provide motivation to tackle more significant challenges.

In essence, mistakes and bad habits serve as both a mirror and window: a mirror reflecting the internal emotional and psychological state and a window into potential strategies for improvement and growth. Overcoming them is less about eradicating negative behaviours and more about holistic self-improvement. Seen this way, mistakes and bad habits transform from burdens into opportunities, turning points that can either lead to a cycle of repetition or a path of self-discovery and growth.

Mistakes and bad habits may not be as dramatic as other mental health issues, but their cumulative effect can be just as damaging. They can contribute to a sense of failure, inadequacy, or lack of control, which in turn can feed into more significant mental struggles. The key to turning these potential pitfalls into opportunities for growth lies in our ability to understand them, to confront them without judgment, and to incorporate them into our more extensive journey of emotional and psychological self-improvement. So, the next time you find yourself grappling with mistakes or entrenched in bad habits, remember: these, too, are part of why your brain may seem like an adversary, but they're also your most straightforward path to turning it into an ally.

MISTAKES AND BAD HABITS

ANGER, FRUSTRATION, and TEMPER

As we navigate the maze of human emotions, we eventually confront the intense, often disruptive feelings of anger, frustration, and temper. These are emotions that don't just add spice to life; they can set the whole kitchen on fire if not properly managed. They can strain relationships, disrupt workplaces, and wreak havoc on our mental well-being. They can help us understand "Why My Brain Hates Me." So, how do we handle these fiery emotions without getting burned? The answer lies in understanding their origins and implementing effective strategies for management and control.

The intense emotions of anger, frustration, and temper are far more than just reactive states; they are the culmination of complex psychological and neurological processes. Each of these emotions, although seemingly spontaneous, has a unique origin and a specific set of triggers that can be traced back to both our cognitive makeup and our physiological responses.

At the root of anger is often a sense of powerlessness or a feeling of injustice. Whether we perceive that we have been wronged or that our

ANGER, FRUSTRATION, AND TEMPER

agency has been compromised, these feelings can quickly escalate into anger. This emotion serves as a psychological alert system, signalling to us that something needs to be addressed or changed. In many ways, anger can act as a call to action, prompting us to rectify the situation that caused the perceived injustice or power imbalance.

Frustration, while closely related to anger, generally originates from a different source: blocked goals or unmet expectations. Whether it's an ambition we can't realize or a desire that goes unfulfilled, the inability to achieve what we aim for leads to a buildup of frustration. This emotion serves as a cognitive signal that our strategy needs re-evaluation, pushing us toward problem-solving and adaptability.

Temper is often seen as the external manifestation of these internal emotional states. It acts as the release valve for pent-up anger and frustration, although not always in a manner that's constructive or socially acceptable.

From a neurological perspective, the amygdala plays a critical role in these intense emotional experiences. Located deep within the temporal lobe of the brain, the amygdala serves as the primary processing center for emotional responses. When this part of the brain detects a threat—whether it's real, like a physical danger, or perceived, such as a social slight—it can trigger a fight-or-flight response. This physiological reaction readies the body for rapid action, which often manifests as anger or a temper outburst.

Understanding the psychological and neurological underpinnings of these intense emotions is not just about gaining academic knowledge. It's a vital part of self-awareness and emotional regulation. Recognizing the root causes and triggers of anger, frustration, and temper can empower us with the tools to manage these emotions more effectively. This deeper understanding enables us to break the cycle of emotional reactivity, providing us with the strategies we need to navigate our emotional landscape more successfully.

When managing intense emotions like anger, a one-size-fits-all approach rarely works. Anger is a complex emotion with various triggers, expressions, and underlying psychological factors. So, how do you keep this volatile emotion in check? The key lies in a toolbox of practical, evidence-based strategies tailored to your unique emotional landscape.

Deep breathing isn't just a cliché; it's a physiologically sound method for calming the nervous system. The next time you find your temper rising, take deep, slow breaths, filling your lungs completely and then exhaling fully. Counting to ten serves a similar purpose—it provides a brief but critical pause that can disrupt the emotional cascade, leading to an outburst. It's like hitting the pause button, giving you a moment to reconsider your next action.

Cognitive reframing is another tool worth wielding. This involves stepping back and re-evaluating the situation, fueling your anger. Is it a personal attack, or is it perhaps a misunderstanding? Is it a deliberate attempt to harm you, or could it be unintentional? By reassessing the situation, you can gain a new perspective that might mitigate your anger.

Physical exercise is another potent tool for anger management. The act of engaging in physical activity—be it a brisk walk, a jog, or even a full-blown workout—can serve as a healthy outlet for your aggression. Exercise releases endorphins, natural mood lifters that can counteract the negative emotional energy of anger. It's like channelling your anger into something constructive, turning destructive potential into a force for good.

The S.T.O.P. technique (Stop, Take a breath, Observe, Proceed) is an acronym to remember when you're in the heat of the moment. When you feel anger rising, stop what you're doing, take a deep breath to give yourself a moment to think, observe what's happening without judgment, and then proceed with a course of action.

ANGER, FRUSTRATION, AND TEMPER

A less discussed but equally important tool is the act of seeking professional help. Sometimes, anger is a symptom of underlying issues that require specialized intervention. Therapists and counsellors can provide more personalized strategies based on cognitive behavioural therapy or other evidence-based treatments.

These tools don't exist in isolation; they can be combined in various ways to suit different situations and emotional states. The key to effective anger management lies in knowing which tool to use when, and like any skill, it gets easier with practice. Over time, as you become more adept at recognizing the early signs of anger and choosing the appropriate tool for the situation, you'll find that what once seemed like an uncontrollable force becomes much more manageable.

The ability to transition from emotional turbulence, such as frustration, to a state of composure is not just a skill but an essential component of emotional intelligence. Achieving this equilibrium allows for better decision-making, improved relationships, and an overall sense of well-being. The challenge lies in learning to regulate emotions effectively, a process that requires deliberate action and thoughtful strategies.

The first critical step in the journey toward emotional composure is identifying the source of your frustration. This could range from external factors like a delayed flight or challenging coworkers to more deeply rooted issues like feelings of inadequacy or existential concerns. Recognizing the root cause helps you move beyond the emotional fog and lends clarity to the situation.

After identifying the source, a problem-solving approach comes into play. Generating a list of potential solutions has a dual benefit: not only does it equip you with possible courses of action, but it also diverts your focus from the problem itself to possible remedies. This change in focus often leads to a reduction in the intensity of the emotion as you begin to see pathways out of the frustrating situation.

Now comes the practical aspect of emotional regulation: implementing coping mechanisms. These strategies are the toolkit you build over time, tailored to your individual preferences and needs. Some people find solace in listening to calming music, which can lower cortisol levels and reduce the physiological symptoms of stress. Others may find mindfulness exercises, such as deep breathing or guided meditation, to be more effective in grounding their emotions. Sharing your concerns with a trusted confidant can also be incredibly cathartic, providing both emotional release and potential solutions you might not have considered.

Moreover, the practice of emotional regulation is not a one-off endeavour but a continuous process. It requires ongoing commitment and the willingness to adapt your strategies as you gain more insights into your emotional triggers and responses. By effectively regulating your emotions, you not only improve your immediate circumstances but also equip yourself with the skills necessary for long-term emotional well-being. This sets the stage for a life characterized not by the avoidance of emotional challenges but by the capability to navigate them with grace and resilience.

There's no denying the potency of anger, frustration, and temper. However, they don't have to dictate the quality of your life. By understanding the psychology behind these intense emotions and implementing practical, evidence-based strategies to manage them, you can transform these potential sources of disruption into catalysts for positive change and personal growth.

In wrapping up this exploration of anger, frustration, and temper, it becomes evident that the journey is not a sprint but a marathon. The roadmap laid out—comprising understanding the underlying psychology, identifying emotional triggers, and implementing tailored coping strategies—serves as a guide. However, the real work lies in the day-to-day application of these principles. The end goal is not to achieve a state of unflappable calm but to build a robust emotional toolkit that

ANGER, FRUSTRATION, AND TEMPER

allows for a more nuanced, mature response to life's inevitable challenges.

The profound impact of successfully managing intense emotions like anger, frustration, and temper extends far beyond the individual. It has a ripple effect on interpersonal relationships, professional life, and overall well-being. It's not just about extinguishing emotional fires as they arise but about creating a psychological environment where these fires are less likely to ignite in the first place. The skills developed in this emotional regulation journey not only defuse immediate crises but also contribute to a broader sense of emotional intelligence, enriching life in all its complexity.

As this chapter concludes, it's worth noting that emotional regulation is not a solitary endeavour. While personal commitment is undeniably crucial, support from trusted individuals and possibly professionals can provide invaluable reinforcement. Emotional well-being is not a destination but an ongoing process, one that continually adapts to new challenges and incorporates new insights. And so, as the intricacies of anger, frustration, and temper are unpacked and understood, the stage is set for a more prosperous, more emotionally balanced life. This is not just emotional management; it's emotional mastery. It's not about limiting emotional experience but enhancing it—turning what could be stumbling blocks into stepping stones on the path to a fuller, more balanced life.

ANXIETY *and* STRESS

In the labyrinth of human emotions, anxiety and stress are often the winding pathways that many of us find challenging to navigate. These are not merely buzzwords or states of mind to be dismissed with a wave of the hand; they are complex psychological phenomena that can significantly influence our quality of life, relationships, and overall well-being. How do we decode these ubiquitous yet often misunderstood emotional states? The key lies in a nuanced understanding of their multiple facets and the impact they exert on our cognitive functions. Understanding anxiety and stress will help us understand "Why My Brain Hates Me."

Anxiety stands as a complex phenomenon, far exceeding the boundaries of simple worry or concern. It's a term frequently thrown around, yet its depth and impact are often underestimated. To truly comprehend anxiety, it's essential to recognize it as a multifaceted experience that transcends mere emotional discomfort, permeating both our physical and cognitive states.

At the emotional level, anxiety manifests as a persistent, often irrational sense of fear or dread. Unlike worry, which tends to be tied to a specific issue or circumstance, anxiety often lacks a clear or immediate trigger. This nebulous nature makes it particularly unsettling; it's a form of distress that seems to envelop us without apparent reason, often leading to feelings of irritability and restlessness. More intense manifestations may even generate an overwhelming sensation of impending doom, a sort of existential angst that doesn't align with the reality of one's circumstances.

However, anxiety doesn't confine itself to the emotional realm; it has significant physical manifestations as well. From heart palpitations and shortness of breath to digestive issues like nausea or irritable bowel syndrome, the body becomes a theatre where anxiety plays out its drama. These physical symptoms are not just side effects but integral aspects of the anxiety experience, often amplifying the emotional symptoms and creating a vicious cycle of distress.

The cognitive impact of anxiety is equally significant. Anxiety can lead to a distortion in cognitive processes, making tasks like concentration, decision-making, and problem-solving exceedingly difficult. It's as though the brain gets caught in a loop of distressing thoughts, making it challenging to direct attention elsewhere. This perpetual state of mental unrest can severely impair one's ability to function effectively in daily life.

Understanding anxiety in this holistic manner—acknowledging its emotional, physical, and cognitive dimensions—offers the first step in managing it effectively. When we see anxiety as more than just an escalated form of worry, we can begin to approach it with the comprehensive strategies it requires. By doing so, we open the door to targeted interventions and coping mechanisms that address not just the symptoms but the underlying complexities of this pervasive mental state.

Stress is a fundamental aspect of human physiology, designed as an adaptive mechanism to help us navigate challenging or dangerous situations. It's the body's alert system, a biological imperative that galvanizes us into action. However, the caveat lies in duration and intensity—while acute stress can be beneficial, chronic stress can wreak havoc on our cognitive and physical health.

When confronted with a stressor, the brain secretes cortisol, a hormone integral to the "fight or flight" response. In short bursts, cortisol can enhance alertness, energy levels, and even immune response. However, chronic secretion of cortisol is another story entirely. Prolonged exposure to this hormone can lead to a host of cognitive impairments, including but not limited to memory issues and decreased cognitive flexibility. On a more severe scale, chronic stress can even contribute to neuronal damage, rendering the brain less resilient and adaptive.

Cognitively, stress can lead to a series of distortions in how we perceive and interpret our environment. For example, the cognitive distortion known as catastrophizing can make a challenging situation seem insurmountable, trapping individuals in a cycle of heightened stress and emotional turmoil. Such distortions not only exacerbate the stress experience but also impair one's ability to problem-solve and make effective decisions.

Moreover, the influence of stress extends into behavioural domains, often driving choices that are counterproductive to cognitive health. Poor dietary choices, substance abuse, and a lack of physical exercise often become the coping mechanisms for chronic stress. These behaviours, in turn, contribute to a vicious cycle, intensifying stress and its cognitive repercussions.

Understanding the full scope of stress—its physiological, cognitive, and behavioural dimensions—gives us the necessary framework to address it effectively. It's crucial to recognize that stress and anxiety are not isolated emotional states but complex psychological phenomena with far-reaching implications for our overall well-being. With a nuanced understanding of their intricate mechanisms, we can formulate targeted strategies not only for effective stress management but also for improving the overall quality of life. Through this holistic approach, we have the opportunity to rewrite our emotional narrative, transforming stress from a persistent adversary into a manageable aspect of the human experience.

While stress and anxiety serve important adaptive functions, helping us navigate complex and challenging environments, their persistence and intensity can become problematic. Managing these emotional states is not about expunging them but moderating their impact on our lives. The objective is to prevent them from evolving into chronic issues that impair cognitive function, emotional well-being, and overall quality of life.

One of the most effective strategies for managing anxiety and stress is Cognitive Behavioural Therapy (CBT). This approach is rooted in the premise that our thoughts, feelings, and behaviours are interconnected. By identifying and challenging distorted thought patterns and beliefs that contribute to anxiety, CBT provides a structured path toward emotional regulation. While seeking professional guidance for CBT is often advised, numerous self-help books and online resources grounded in this therapy provide a more accessible avenue for those who prefer to take matters into their own hands.

Mindfulness is another potent tool in the stress and anxiety management arsenal. Originating from ancient meditative practices, modern mindfulness techniques focus on anchoring the mind in the present moment, thereby reducing the rumination and worry that feed stress and anxiety. Simple exercises like focused breathing or body scanning can be incorporated into your daily routine, offering immediate and sustained relief.

Exercise, often underutilized, is a powerful method for managing stress and anxiety. Regular physical activity has a dual effect: it reduces cortisol levels, the hormone associated with stress, while also releasing endorphins, which act as natural mood lifters. The American Heart Association recommends at least 150 minutes of moderate exercise per week, which translates to roughly 30 minutes a day, five times a week. This could be as simple as a brisk walk, a short run, or a session of aerobic exercise.

Social support plays a critical role in emotional well-being. Interpersonal relationships can serve as a buffer against stress and anxiety, providing emotional sustenance and often contributing fresh perspectives on troubling issues. Therefore, it's important to identify a reliable social support network—be it family, friends, or mental health professionals—that you can turn to when the emotional landscape becomes challenging. Sometimes, merely knowing that someone is available to listen can provide immense relief.

Armed with these strategies, you can create a personalized toolkit for managing stress and anxiety. The aim is to create a balanced emotional landscape where these states can exist without overwhelming your daily life, allowing you to function at your best both cognitively and emotionally.

A life without overwhelming stress and anxiety is not merely a theoretical construct or a narrative from self-help books—it's a genuine possibility that can be achieved through continuous effort, self-awareness, and the application of evidence-based strategies. It's a life where stress and anxiety exist but are managed to a degree that they don't impede your daily activities, your relationships, or your overall well-being.

One of the most noteworthy benefits of successfully managing stress and anxiety is the development of emotional resilience. This form of psychological fortitude allows you to face life's adversities with a balanced emotional response. You're not impervious to hardships; instead, you're better equipped to process them, adapt, and move forward. Emotional resilience is like an inner shield that protects you from the extreme swings of life's pendulum, giving you the strength to bounce back from setbacks without getting trapped in a spiral of negative emotions.

Your interpersonal relationships can flourish when you're not overwhelmed by stress or anxiety. A constant state of stress often makes you irritable, less patient, and less attentive to the emotional needs of others. In contrast, effective management of these emotional states can enhance your ability to communicate, empathize, and connect. This has a cascading positive effect on relationships, whether they be romantic partnerships, friendships, or professional associations. The quality of your relationships is a significant determinant of your overall well-being, and by managing your emotional states, you pave the way for more prosperous, more rewarding interactions with others.

It's well-documented that chronic stress and anxiety can have detrimental effects on physical health. Elevated cortisol levels can exacerbate conditions such as hypertension digestive issues, and can even compromise immune function. By keeping stress and anxiety in check, you stand to improve various aspects of your physical health, possibly reducing the need for medication or medical intervention for stress-related ailments. This creates a positive feedback loop; better physical health can, in turn, reduce stress and anxiety, creating a cycle of improvement that contributes to a robust state of overall health.

Unmanaged stress and anxiety often become barriers to opportunities. They can make you hesitant to take risks or seize initiatives that could lead to career advancement or personal growth. However, when these emotional states are well-managed, you find the mental space to seek out and grab hold of opportunities. Your decision-making becomes less clouded, your focus sharpens, and your ability to handle complex tasks improves. This leads to a more fulfilling career better job performance, and opens doors to experiences that contribute to personal growth and happiness.

A profound sense of well-being without being overwhelmed is at the core of a life. This is not merely the absence of negative states but the presence of positive ones. You experience joy more fully, engage more deeply in activities, and find a greater sense of purpose. This well-being extends beyond yourself to positively influence your interactions with others and the environment. It forms the basis for a content, fulfilling life characterized by a deep-seated happiness that isn't easily shaken by external events.

It's important to note that managing stress and anxiety is not a one-time achievement but a continuous process. It's akin to maintaining physical fitness; you don't reach your desired state and then abandon all efforts. Instead, you continue to apply the strategies that got you there, adapting them as needed to meet new challenges. Even setbacks become part of the learning curve, opportunities to refine your approach and become more skilled at managing your emotional landscape.

The possibility of a life without overwhelming, marked by emotional resilience, fulfilling relationships, and a deep sense of well-being, is not just a pipe dream. It's a realistic goal that can be achieved with commitment, self-awareness, and the application of effective strategies for managing stress and anxiety. It's a life where challenges are met with equanimity, relationships are nurtured through empathy and clear communication, and the joy of existence is felt more keenly.

Through a multi-pronged approach that includes cognitive behavioural techniques, mindfulness practices, physical exercise, and a robust social support system, this balanced state of existence is attainable. It's a lifelong endeavour but one that promises an enriching, rewarding life that is lived to its fullest potential.

In drawing this section to a close, the essence that emerges is one of sustainable well-being, a state achieved not through the absence of difficulties but through the mastery of coping strategies that make life's challenges manageable and even enriching. The journey toward a life without overwhelm is not a linear path free from obstacles; rather, it's a spiral that may include setbacks and detours but always leads upward toward greater emotional resilience and more profound satisfaction.

This sense of well-being—encompassing both the emotional and the physical, the personal and the interpersonal—becomes the lens through which life is viewed. It transforms the narrative from one of surviving to one of thriving. The tools and strategies discussed—ranging from mindfulness and cognitive behavioural techniques to maintaining physical health and cultivating a robust social network—are not just reactive measures for moments of crisis but proactive steps toward building a life of fulfillment and meaning.

The idea is not to eliminate stress and anxiety, which are inevitable facets of human experience, but to modulate and manage them in a way that contributes to, rather than detracts from, the richness of life. They become teachers rather than tormentors, providing valuable insights into personal limitations and areas for growth.

It's a dynamic process, ever-evolving and adapting to life's changing circumstances. Yet, the core principle remains: a life without overwhelm is not a utopian fantasy but a practical aspiration. With commitment and consistent effort, it's more than possible; it's probable. This journey is less about the destination and more about how the path is navigated. As this intricate navigation becomes second nature, the true reward is unveiled: a life imbued with a level of depth, meaning, and joy that not only enriches one's own existence but also positively influences that of others. Thus, the quest for a life without overwhelm transcends individual benefit, becoming a gift to everyone in its orbit.

WHY MY BRAIN *hates* ME?

We've all had moments when it feels like our brain is our worst enemy. Whether it's persistent negative thoughts, crippling anxiety, or the inability to focus when we most need to, it can be frustrating and disheartening to feel like the very organ that makes us who we are is sabotaging our happiness and well-being. But is our brain working against us? Or is it a matter of understanding its complexities and learning how to harness its powers for our benefit?

Understanding why we sometimes feel as though our brain is working against us requires a nuanced exploration of various interrelated factors. This notion—that our brain seems to be our adversary rather than our ally—is far from a baseless feeling; it is rooted in biological, psychological, and environmental factors that all converge to influence our emotional landscape.

First and foremost, it's essential to recognize that the human brain is hardwired for survival, not for happiness. This is a critical distinction that has far-reaching implications for our emotional well-being. The brain's primary function is to keep us alive and to do so, it has developed various mechanisms for identifying threats. One such mechanism is the "negativity bias," a cognitive and emotional inclination to focus more on negative circumstances than on positive ones. This bias served us well when survival was a daily struggle, where overlooking a threat could be fatal. However, in our modern, relatively safe environment, this negativity bias often misfires, leading us to stress over traffic jams and office politics as if they were life-or-death situations. The result is an ongoing state of heightened stress and anxiety, where negative thoughts take center stage.

Closely related to this is the role of neurotransmitters like serotonin and dopamine, which are chemical messengers in the brain that help regulate mood, among other things. Imbalances in these neurotransmitters can cause emotional turbulence, manifesting as persistent sadness, heightened anxiety, or even clinical depression. The regulation of these neurotransmitters is influenced by a variety of factors, including diet, physical activity, sleep, and stress. Any imbalance in these areas can disrupt the delicate equilibrium of these neurotransmitters, leading to emotional states that feel uncontrollable.

Environmental factors add another layer of complexity. Our upbringing, the culture we are raised in, our life experiences, and even our current circumstances all contribute to shaping our emotional landscape. Traumatic experiences, either in childhood or later in life, can have a particularly lasting impact. These emotional scars can persist long after the events have passed, influencing how we perceive the world, think, and feel. It's not just traumatic events that have this power; even daily, chronic stressors like a toxic work environment or a strained relationship can gradually shape our cognitive habits toward negativity.

This brings us to cognitive habits or thought patterns we've developed over the years or even decades. These patterns can become so deeply ingrained that they occur automatically, without conscious thought. Such automatic negative thoughts can contribute to feelings of despair, hopelessness, or chronic negativity. These thought patterns are often self-reinforcing, creating a vicious cycle that can be difficult to break.

Understanding the 'why' behind these emotions and thoughts is the first critical step in changing the narrative. It requires a multi-dimensional approach that may involve medical intervention for neurotransmitter imbalances, cognitive-behavioural therapy to change long-standing thought patterns, lifestyle changes to mitigate environmental stressors, or, more likely, a combination of all these factors.

It's crucial to recognize that your brain doesn't hate you. It's doing its job based on the information and resources it has. Your brain's seeming betrayal is not an act of malice but a consequence of its primary function skewed by modern life's complexities and challenges. And just as the brain can learn to adapt to negative patterns, it can also adapt to positive ones. With the right tools, resources, and support, you can retrain your brain to work for you rather than against you.

So, the next time you feel like your brain is your enemy, remember that it is a complex organ influenced by a multitude of factors. You have the power to change that relationship. By acknowledging the factors that contribute to your emotional state, you equip yourself with the knowledge to take actionable steps toward improvement. This self-awareness, coupled with appropriate intervention strategies, can turn your brain from a seeming adversary into a powerful ally in your journey toward better mental and emotional well-being.

In summary, feeling like your brain is against you is not a sign of personal failure or an unchangeable reality. It's a complex issue with roots in biology, psychology, and environment, and it's a starting point for positive change. By understanding the 'why,' you can begin the process of transforming your emotional life, turning your brain into an ally and making it a cornerstone of your well-being rather than an obstacle to it.

Finding oneself in a state of mental disarray or feeling at odds with one's own mind is a common, albeit discomforting, experience. It's akin to living in a house where the walls seem to close in on you or being in a relationship where you don't understand your partner's actions—except that you're both the house and the inhabitant, the relationship and both parties involved. The good news is that reconciliation is possible; it starts with understanding the internal dynamics that govern your thoughts, emotions, and actions.

The process of reconciliation with your mind is a multi-step journey that commences with self-awareness. One cannot change what one does not understand. Therefore, the first critical step is to become intimately acquainted with your own thought patterns, emotional triggers, and behavioural tendencies. One effective way to achieve this is through journaling. The act of writing down your thoughts can be illuminating; it serves as a mirror, reflecting the complexities of your mind that might not be immediately apparent. Another method is mindful contemplation—taking out a few quiet moments daily to just sit and observe your thoughts without judgment. These practices don't aim to change your thoughts but to understand them, which is the first step toward meaningful change.

It helps you realize that you are not your thoughts and that you don't have to react to them. This awareness creates a mental space that allows you to choose your responses rather than being impulsively driven by your thoughts and emotions. The techniques range from simple breathing exercises to more complex forms of meditation. But the essence remains the same: be present and observe without judgment.

The process of reconciling with your mind is neither quick nor straightforward. It requires patience and consistent effort and often involves a combination of multiple approaches—from introspection and psychotherapy to physical exercise and proper nutrition. It is an ongoing process of understanding and managing your internal landscape. When you implement these strategies, you're not just resolving the discord with your mind; you're laying the foundation for a more harmonious life.

In doing so, you'll find that making peace with your mind transforms not only your internal world but also profoundly enriches your external experiences. You'll navigate your relationships, your work, and even your leisure activities with a newfound sense of clarity and purpose. In essence, by reconciling with your mind, you open the door to a more fulfilling, meaningful, and peaceful life.

The relationship we have with our brains is perhaps one of the most consequential yet overlooked aspects of our lives. Many people operate under the assumption that their brains are fixed entities, hardwired to think, feel, and react in predetermined ways. This mindset can foster a relationship of adversity with one's brain, especially when experiencing negative thoughts, emotional struggles, or mental health challenges. However, neuroscience and psychology tell a different, more empowering story—one where the brain is not an adversary but a potential ally. Transforming this relationship from one of discord to one of partnership is no small task, but the rewards are not only attainable; they are profoundly life-changing.

Understanding neuroplasticity is a pivotal starting point. Neuroplasticity refers to the brain's remarkable ability to change and adapt throughout a person's life. It's the mechanism through which all learning and memory occur. Knowing that your brain is capable of such flexibility can be incredibly empowering. It means the power to change lies in external factors and within you. Every experience you engage in, every book you read, every new skill you learn, and even every thought you think contributes to reshaping your neural pathways. You're not just a passive recipient of neural wiring; you're an active participant in its ongoing transformation.

To leverage this transformative potential, actionable steps are crucial. One effective strategy is journaling. By tracking your thoughts, emotions, and reactions, you can identify patterns that might be contributing to a negative mindset or emotional state. Writing things down externalizes them, making them easier to analyze. You can pinpoint triggers for stress, anxiety, or depressive thoughts and begin to understand how to approach these triggers differently. Journaling also allows you to celebrate small victories—a day without succumbing to negative thoughts. This successful interaction would have previously triggered anxiety or even a moment of unexpected happiness or peace.

Surrounding yourself with positive influences is a crucial step. The environments we inhabit and the people we interact with have significant impacts on our mental well-being. If you're constantly surrounded by negativity, it will be challenging to rewire your brain for positivity. This might mean making difficult decisions, like distancing yourself from toxic relationships or disengaging from harmful environments. On the flip side, intentionally spending time in positive environments—whether that means more time in nature, joining a group or organization that aligns with your values, or engaging in activities that bring you joy—can have a transformative effect on your mental landscape.

A commitment to lifelong learning is another powerful tool in your arsenal. The act of learning does more than just arm you with new information or skills; it fundamentally changes your brain, enhancing its cognitive flexibility. This makes your brain more resilient to stress and better equipped to adapt to new challenges or setbacks. Whether it's taking up a new hobby, diving into a subject matter you're passionate about, or pursuing a new career path, the benefits extend beyond the acquisition of new knowledge to a more profound, structural level of brain transformation.

Professional guidance can also provide invaluable perspectives. Psychologists, therapists, life coaches, and even career advisors can offer insights into aligning your mental patterns with your life goals. Their external perspectives can help you recognize thought patterns and emotional reactions that you might not be aware of. They can also provide targeted strategies for mental well-being, from cognitive-behavioral techniques to mindfulness practices.

The transition from seeing your brain as an adversary to an ally is not an overnight transformation. It's a sustained effort that requires a multi-pronged approach. Medical, psychological, and lifestyle changes are all pieces of this complex puzzle. But as they say, the journey of a thousand miles begins with a single step. Each small victory, each positive change, and each moment of clarity or peace is a step toward a more symbiotic relationship with your brain. Over time, these steps add up, leading you toward a more fulfilling, balanced, and harmonious life.

In conclusion, the relationship with your brain doesn't have to be one of struggle and strife. By understanding the mechanisms that make transformation possible and taking actionable steps to effect that change, you can turn what might have been an adversary into one of your greatest allies. It's a long journey, but it's one that holds the promise of a more prosperous, more fulfilling life. And that is a journey unquestionably worth taking.

UNHEALTHY DESIRES, ADDICTIONS, *and* CRAVINGS

We all have desires, cravings, and even addictions to some extent. They range from the benign to the detrimental, shaping our choices, lifestyles, and, ultimately, our well-being. But when do these urges cross the line from ordinary human experiences to unhealthy compulsions that undermine our health and happiness? This chapter delves into the intricate web of desires, addictions, and cravings, offering insights into their origins, manifestations, and the steps we can take to manage them effectively. This helps us understand "Why My Brain Hates Me."

When understanding human behaviour, the role of desire cannot be underestimated. As a motivating force, desire propels us to achieve goals, seek pleasure, and even avoid pain. But the question remains: Where do desires come from? The answer to this question is multifaceted, encompassing biological, psychological, and sociocultural dimensions.

UNHEALTHY DESIRES, ADDICTIONS, AND CRAVINGS

Biologically, desire has its roots in the brain's complex reward system, where neurotransmitters like dopamine play a crucial role. In simple terms, whenever we engage in an activity that is essential for survival or brings pleasure, dopamine is released, signalling to our brain that this is something worth repeating. This biological mechanism was evolutionarily advantageous for activities like finding food or a suitable mate. However, in the modern world, this system can be hijacked by less than advantageous pursuits, such as addictive behaviors or the consumption of unhealthy foods. This biological factor explains why we may desire things that give us immediate gratification but are not necessarily good for us in the long run.

From a psychological perspective, desires often stem from emotional needs or deficiencies. We might desire companionship, love, or even recognition from others. These psychological motivations are shaped by our individual experiences, including our upbringing, relationships, and even the challenges we've faced in our lives. In many ways, our past shapes what we desire in the present and future. Our emotional history, self-esteem, and psychological needs can all define the landscape of our desires.

Sociocultural factors further shape our desires. We live in societies with norms, values, and expectations that often dictate what is desirable. This is most apparent in the way advertising and media influence our wants. External forces are powerful shapers of desire, whether it's the type of body we should have, the lifestyle we aspire to, or the status symbols we should own. Social media platforms, in particular, amplify this effect by creating a continuous loop of comparison, aspiration, and, ultimately, desire.

While desire is a natural aspect of the human experience, addictions and cravings represent a darker, more intense form of this experience. Unlike desires, which can be healthy or at least neutral, addictions are often destructive, affecting not just the individual but also those around them.

Neurobiologically, addictions are rooted in the same reward system that drives desire. However, in the case of addiction, this system is not just activated but altered. The release of dopamine, which usually signals pleasure, becomes an overwhelming drive that dominates an individual's thoughts and actions. In other words, the brain's reward system becomes hyper-responsive, creating an urgency that's difficult to control. This transformation is particularly pronounced in the case of substance abuse, where the chemical interaction with the brain exacerbates the addiction but can also occur with behaviours like gambling, eating, or even internet usage.

Environmental factors also play a pivotal role in the development of addiction. Whether it's exposure to addictive substances, societal pressures, or emotional trauma, external circumstances can act as triggers. For instance, someone who grows up in an environment where substance abuse is normalized may be more susceptible to similar behaviour. Emotional traumas, often stemming from early life experiences, can also contribute to addiction as individuals may use substances or behaviours as coping mechanisms.

Moreover, specific individuals are more predisposed to addiction due to genetic factors or co-occurring mental health conditions like depression and anxiety. There's also evidence to suggest that adverse experiences in childhood, such as neglect or abuse, can make individuals more susceptible to addiction later in life. In these instances, addiction can be seen as a symptom of a more significant psychological or emotional issue.

Understanding the origins of desire, addiction, and cravings provides more than just academic knowledge; it offers a roadmap for intervention and self-improvement. By recognizing the multi-dimensional roots of these experiences, we can tailor strategies to manage them effectively. This could mean addressing underlying emotional issues, restructuring our environment to minimize triggers, or even seeking medical help for a biological predisposition to addiction.

UNHEALTHY DESIRES, ADDICTIONS, AND CRAVINGS

In conclusion, desires, addictions, and cravings are complex phenomena that arise from a confluence of biological, psychological, and environmental factors. Understanding these various dimensions is crucial for individual well-being and broader societal health. It equips us with the knowledge to differentiate between healthy and unhealthy desires. It offers a foundational understanding that can be the first step toward effective intervention and long-lasting change.

The terms "addictions" and "cravings" may often be conflated or used interchangeably in casual conversation, but from a clinical perspective, they represent distinct psychological and physiological phenomena. Understanding the nuanced differences between these terms not only offers clarity but also provides a lens through which we can examine and address these complex issues.

In the medical and psychological fields, addiction is generally understood as a chronic condition characterized by an inability to stop using a substance or engaging in a behaviour despite the negative consequences it incurs. It's a multi-dimensional issue, often requiring a multi-faceted approach to treatment, encompassing pharmacological, psychological, and even social interventions. Addiction is not a sign of moral failure or a lack of willpower; instead, it is increasingly recognized as a complex interplay of neurochemical, psychological, and environmental factors.

While substances like drugs and alcohol are often the first things to come to mind when discussing addiction, behavioural addictions such as gambling, eating disorders, and excessive internet use are also actual and can be equally damaging. In fact, the American Psychiatric Association has included gambling disorder in its Diagnostic and Statistical Manual of Mental Disorders (DSM-5), solidifying its status as a behavioural addiction. What ties these different forms of addiction together is the compulsive, almost involuntary nature of the behaviour and its detrimental effects on the individual's physical and mental health, relationships, and overall well-being.

Cravings, on the other hand, are intense urges or desires to use a substance or engage in a specific behaviour. Unlike addiction, which is a sustained and long-term condition, cravings are acute, short-term experiences. They are typically more episodic, coming in waves, and are often triggered by specific cues or situations. Cravings can occur in a variety of contexts, ranging from hunger for a particular item of food to the urge to smoke a cigarette. They are not inherently indicative of addiction, although they are a common symptom of addictive disorders. For example, someone who is trying to quit smoking might experience intense cravings when exposed to a trigger like stress or the sight of someone else smoking.

Importantly, cravings can also act as a gateway to relapse for those in recovery from addiction. The brain has a remarkable capacity for associative learning, which means that it can associate specific cues or contexts with the pleasurable effects of substance use or typical behaviour. This association can make cravings exceptionally hard to manage for those who are trying to abstain from addictive behaviour. Thus, an integral part of addiction treatment often involves teaching individuals strategies to manage or cope with cravings.

Both addictions and cravings exploit the brain's reward system, a series of neural pathways that evolved to reinforce behaviours essential for survival, like eating and reproduction. However, this system can be co-opted by substances and behaviours that provide intense, immediate pleasure but have long-term detrimental effects. When the reward system is hijacked in this manner, it can override rational decision-making processes, leading individuals to engage in behaviours that are contrary to their long-term well-being.

The distinction between addictions and cravings often lies in their duration, intensity, and the individual's level of control over these urges. Cravings are generally shorter-lived and can often be managed through conscious effort or avoidance strategies. Addictions, however, are more

UNHEALTHY DESIRES, ADDICTIONS, AND CRAVINGS

enduring and pervasive and frequently require external intervention for effective management.

While cravings and addictions may share similarities, notably their exploitation of the brain's reward system, they differ significantly in their duration, impact, and treatability. Understanding these differences is crucial for clinicians, policymakers, and individuals as they navigate the intricate and often challenging landscape of human desire, impulse control, and behavioural health. By clearly defining and distinguishing these terms, we can better identify, treat, and perhaps even prevent the negative outcomes associated with them.

While desires, cravings, and even mild forms of addiction can be a normal part of the human experience, there exists a threshold where these urges become detrimental to our well-being. But how do we distinguish between what's healthy and what's not?

Unhealthy desires often manifest as obsessive thoughts, taking up an inordinate amount of mental space and leading to actions that harm oneself or others. They may involve substances, like drugs or alcohol, or behaviors, like excessive eating or gambling.

Addictions and cravings become unhealthy when they meet certain criteria, such as interfering with daily activities or responsibilities, leading to deteriorating health, either physical or mental. Also, causing harm to oneself or others, resulting in a loss of control or ability to stop despite wanting to.

Necessitating increased amounts of a substance or activity to achieve the desired effect, indicative of tolerance, and leading to withdrawal symptoms when the substance or activity is not available—these are also some of the unhealthy aspects of addiction.

Understanding the characteristics that delineate unhealthy desires, addictions, and cravings from their healthier counterparts is the first step in addressing the issue. This knowledge equips us to recognize problematic patterns in ourselves or others and seek intervention when necessary.

When delving into the psychology of cravings and unhealthy desires, we find that these urges are often rooted in a combination of factors, both psychological and biological. Sometimes, our bodies crave what they lack; for example, a deficiency in certain minerals can trigger cravings for foods that contain those nutrients. More often, though, our cravings are less about physical need and more about emotional comfort. Emotionally charged situations can trigger cravings as a coping mechanism, providing temporary relief from stress, sadness, or anxiety. At times, even boredom can trigger cravings as the brain seeks stimulation.

However, understanding the origin of cravings and desires doesn't fully explain why we sometimes act against our better judgment. The field of behavioural psychology offers insights here, pointing to the fact that humans are not always rational beings, especially when immediate gratification clashes with long-term well-being. The brain's reward system is wired to prioritize immediate rewards over delayed benefits, a trait that served us well in our early history but complicates our lives today.

So, why do we make unhealthy choices, and what are some typical examples of these? The answer often lies in the complex interplay between our emotional state, environment, and the immediate rewards we seek. Unhealthy choices can manifest in various ways, from opting for high-sugar, high-fat foods when stressed to engaging in risky behaviours like excessive alcohol consumption or drug use. For others, it may be compulsive shopping, binge-watching television, or neglecting physical activity. The reasons for making these choices often boil down to a desire for immediate relief or pleasure without regard for the long-term consequences.

UNHEALTHY DESIRES, ADDICTIONS, AND CRAVINGS

Environmental triggers and social influences also contribute to unhealthy decision-making. If you're at a party where everyone is drinking, the social pressure might make it more challenging to abstain. Likewise, your emotional state, heavily influenced by stressors like work pressure or personal issues, can push you toward making choices you might later regret.

Recognizing these patterns is the first step toward making healthier decisions. By understanding the psychological and situational factors that lead to unhealthy choices, we are better equipped to disrupt these patterns, opting for behaviours that align with our long-term goals and well-being.

Change is seldom easy, especially when it involves deep-seated desires and long-standing habits. However, the path to loving oneself often necessitates these difficult changes. The good news is it's entirely possible, and the rewards are invaluable. Changing for the better starts with a conscious commitment to understanding oneself and making proactive choices that align with one's well-being.

One of the most effective strategies for transformation is mindfulness. By becoming fully aware of your cravings and triggers in real time, you're better equipped to manage them. Instead of succumbing to a craving, pause and consider its source, and evaluate whether giving in will serve your long-term well-being. This moment of awareness can be the difference between making a choice you'll regret and one that aligns with your goals.

By identifying negative thought patterns and learning to challenge them, you can develop healthier beliefs and behaviours that contribute to self-love. Professional guidance from a therapist or counsellor can offer tailored advice and coping strategies specific to your situation.

In summing up, the journey toward making healthier choices is a multifaceted endeavour rooted in self-awareness, environmental understanding, and mindful decision-making. The endeavour is complex but not insurmountable. The key lies in transforming an intricate web of emotional triggers, environmental pressures, and deeply ingrained habits into a coherent strategy for well-being. The transition from unhealthy choices to healthier ones is not a binary switch but a continuum of incremental changes, each contributing to a more holistic sense of self-love and long-term well-being.

The tools for this transformation—mindfulness, cognitive reframing, and professional guidance—serve as navigational aids on this journey. They are not quick fixes but lifelong companions that help refine the decision-making process, making it more attuned to long-term goals rather than immediate gratification. It's a form of internal governance guiding emotional and cognitive processes toward choices that align with an envisioned healthier self.

The ultimate reward for this painstaking process is not just an absence of regret but a positive, proactive form of self-love that manifests in every choice made—choices that nourish the body, enrich the mind, and fulfill the spirit. This culminates in a state of well-being that is robust, resilient, and adaptive, capable of meeting life's varied challenges with a balanced, healthy response.

In the grand scheme of things, the objective is not just to make better choices but to become a better decision-maker whose actions consistently reflect a commitment to sustained well-being and self-love. It's not just about surviving the challenges but thriving amidst them, transforming each obstacle into a stepping stone towards a more prosperous, more fulfilling life. This, in essence, is the ultimate goal: a life where each choice, no matter how small, is a conscious step toward a greater, more loving self.

UNHEALTHY DESIRES, ADDICTIONS, AND CRAVINGS

SELF-LOVE

The journey to self-love is an ongoing process, laden with challenges but ripe with opportunities for growth and fulfillment. By recognizing unhealthy patterns and taking concrete steps to change, you embark on a lifelong journey toward improved well-being and, most importantly, a loving relationship with yourself.

Self-love isn't an endpoint; it's a process, a continuous evolution that asks for your active participation, vulnerability, and courage. The landscape of self-love is both internal and external, impacting not just the way you feel about yourself but also how you interact with the world around you. It's the cornerstone upon which you build relationships, establish your career, and define your purpose and happiness.

Historically, self-love has been misunderstood often mischaracterized as narcissism, selfishness, or an inflated sense of self. However, authentic self-love is far from these misconceptions. It is about understanding your worth and value, and it manifests in the choices you make, the boundaries you set, and the priorities you establish. It's about acknowledging both your strengths and weaknesses and moving forward with the understanding that both contribute to who you are. It's the balance between self-acceptance and self-improvement.

Recognizing unhealthy patterns is often the first and most crucial step in the journey toward self-love. Unhealthy patterns could be anything from negative self-talk, procrastination, or self-doubt to more destructive behaviours like substance abuse or self-harm. The power lies in not just identifying these patterns but also understanding their roots. Is your negative self-talk a result of a past relationship? Does your procrastination stem from a fear of failure? Identifying the underlying factors gives you the insight needed to challenge these patterns and replace them with healthier alternatives.

One of the most impactful ways to cultivate self-love is through mindfulness. This practice enables you to become an observer of your thoughts and feelings, providing the space to question, challenge, and change them. Mindfulness helps you realize that you are not your thoughts; you are the observer of your thoughts. This distinction, though subtle, is incredibly empowering. It offers the freedom to choose how you respond to your thoughts, enabling a proactive rather than reactive approach to life's challenges.

Another critical element in the journey to self-love is the practice of self-compassion. This means treating yourself with the same kindness, concern, and understanding you would offer to a good friend. Instead of mercilessly judging and criticizing yourself for various inadequacies or shortcomings, self-compassion means you are kind and understanding when confronted with personal failings.

Seeking professional guidance can also be invaluable in the quest for self-love. Therapy offers a non-judgmental space to explore your thoughts, feelings, and behaviours, helping you to dig deeper into your emotional triggers and thought patterns. The objective perspective of a therapist can offer invaluable insights into your character and actions, providing tailored coping strategies that pave the way for self-improvement and, ultimately, self-love.

Moreover, as you grow in your journey toward self-love, you'll find that your relationships with others start to change. You'll attract and be attracted to people who genuinely value you. You'll find the courage to move away from toxic environments and relationships that don't serve your well-being. You'll become a better friend, partner, parent, or sibling because loving yourself teaches you how to love others better.

Finally, it's important to remember that self-love is not a destination but a journey filled with ups and downs. There will be setbacks, but these are not failures; they are opportunities for growth. Each challenge offers a lesson, a chance to learn more about who you are and how you relate to the world around you. With each lesson, you become a little stronger, a little wiser, and a little more loving toward yourself.

In conclusion, the journey to self-love is a transformative process that starts with self-awareness, flourishes through mindful practices like self-compassion, and often benefits from professional guidance. It's a deeply personal, lifelong commitment that promises not just a better relationship with oneself but a richer, more meaningful life. While the path may be fraught with challenges, each obstacle presents an opportunity for growth and reaffirmation of your worth. It's a path worth walking, for the destination is nothing less than a life lived to its fullest potential, enriched by the profound, sustaining power of self-love.

CONCLUSION

This book has embarked on an intricate exploration of the human mind and its complexities, from the neurobiology that governs our thoughts, emotions, and behaviours to the psychological battles we face daily. The brain's influence is profound, shaping our moods, emotions, and feelings and exerting control over what we think, how we feel, and what we learn. It's a powerhouse of capabilities and a source of immense challenges, often leading us to ask, "Why does my brain seem to hate me?"

We've delved into the mechanics of how the brain controls and processes emotions, shedding light on what emotions are, their origins, and how our brain governs us. Importantly, we've also explored the benefits of emotional regulation, providing strategies for controlling negative emotions and improving our lives.

Understanding the nuances of control has been pivotal. We've examined how the brain governs our thoughts, feelings, and learning experiences, acknowledging both the positives and negatives of control. We've also highlighted the importance of learning as an academic exercise and a pathway to emotional well-being and cognitive flexibility.

CONCLUSION

We've tackled the emergence of thoughts, their origins, and how they can be shaped for better outcomes. The internal battles we face in our minds, often marked by negative thinking, have been dissected, and strategies for overcoming these struggles, like mind mapping and other cognitive techniques, have been presented.

Insecurities, lack of confidence, and low self-esteem are prevalent issues that many grapple with. We've explored their origins and offered evidence-based tools for overcoming these challenges, emphasizing self-improvement through practical means. Similarly, we've looked at the origins of negative thinking and strategies for its transformation. We've also examined the complex spectrum of human emotions, including regrets, mistakes, flaws, and weaknesses, providing actionable advice for emotional and psychological growth.

Anger, frustration, belligerence, and temper stand as intense emotions that can derail our well-being. We've explored their origins and offered practical tools for management. Likewise, anxiety and stress, often misunderstood, were examined in detail, focusing on their cognitive impact and offering science-backed strategies for their management.

For those grappling with more severe conditions like schizophrenia and psychosis, the book sought to demystify these disorders, delving into their realities beyond societal stereotypes and misunderstandings. Treatment and coping strategies were discussed, as well as the importance of a robust support network.

The book also ventured into the realm of unhealthy desires, addictions, and cravings. These complex issues were broken down into their psychological, biological, and sociocultural origins, with a focus on transforming unhealthy desires and choices into a lifestyle conducive to self-love and improved well-being.

In closing, the path to reconciliation with our brains involves a multi-faceted approach. It's a journey of understanding, acceptance, and proactive management. By implementing the strategies and insights offered in this book, the hope is that you can transform your relationship with your brain from one of adversity to one of partnership, leading to a life of greater peace, understanding, and happiness.

www.ingramcontent.com/pod-product-compliance
Lightning Source LLC
Chambersburg PA
CBHW010448010526
44118CB00019B/2515